# Overcoming Resistance: Success in Counseling Men

by

George A. Harris, Ph.D.

Bobbie L. Huskey, President
James A. Gondles, Jr., Executive Director
Karen L. Kushner, Director of Communications and Publications
Alice Fins, Managing Editor
Jill Furniss, Associate Editor
Mike Selby, Designer and Production Editor

Special thanks to Janet Van Lone Trieschman, Maryland College of Art and Design instructor, for her help.

ISBN 1-56991-032-4

This publication may be ordered from:
American Correctional Association
4380 Forbes Boulevard
Lanham, MD 20706-4322
1-800-825-BOOK

Library of Congress Cataloging-in-Publication Data

Harris, George A., 1950-
    Overcoming treatment resistance: success in counseling men /
George A. Harris.
        p.   cm
    Includes bibliographical references.
    ISBN 1-56991-032-4 (pbk.)
    1.  Therapeutic alliance.  2. Men—counseling of.  3. Resistance
(Psychoanalysis)  4. Psychotherapist and patient.  5. Involuntary
treatment.  I. Title.
RC489.T66H37  1995
616.89'14--dc20                                    95-35032
                                                        CIP

# Table of Contents

# Introduction

*A* major challenge that counselors face is attempting to counsel people who do not want counseling. These so-called treatment-resistant clients present counselors with a unique opportunity to develop their skills and find new approaches to reach these difficult clients.

Dr. Harris outlines some approaches that work. He points out that the counselor must be aware of men's issues and understand the client's basis for resistance. Then, the counselor must be alert to find culturally appropriate approaches. Such sensitivity is a critical component in building the trust that is necessary for the counseling relationship to succeed.

Not only does Harris fill the gap in what counselors are taught in college psychology and counseling courses, but he provides provocative exercises that will be useful for both practitioners and students in the field. This work should have a long life as part of a continuing education program in corrections or as a text for a college course.

ACA believes that counselors and others in the correctional environment can make a significant difference in the lives of individuals. Most individuals can benefit from counseling. This work provides counselors and other therapists with the skills and approaches to do their jobs.

James A. Gondles, Jr.
ACA Executive Director

# Preface

*I*ncreasingly, counselors are recognizing the special problems of counseling men. This work explores men's issues and shows how important they are to counseling those who resist entering treatment. While more women than men seek psychotherapy services, no one thinks that men have fewer problems than women. However, a man's reaction to his problems often is based on being male. So, it is important to understand why men decline to participate in treatment and how they react when forced into treatment. Such an understanding will enable counselors—both male and female—to do a more effective job in helping their clients.

Intuitively, counselors recognize that many clients labeled "treatment resistant" are male, and a disproportionate number of these are African-American. Consider the demographic make-up of prisoners, probationers and parolees, batterers, and drug and alcohol abusers. We also need to consider the problem of the African-American male referred to treatment programs where there are few black therapists.

Men may struggle with cynicism (another topic we discuss) more than women. This may be a reflection of the defenses men use to deal with their life's dilemmas and the special binds that society places on them. Ask any practicing counselor about the wall of cynicism that Vietnam veterans, African-American men, working-class men, and even professional men display; often they distrust counseling as a useless exchange of words.

Yet, as counselors know, before counseling can be effective, the client must have some willingness to participate and some faith that the process can be helpful, despite the fact that those attitudes are all too often absent. Therefore, this work explores the relationship between men's roles, cynicism, and their reluctance to be in counseling and provides a way that both new and experienced counselors can achieve success with these clients.

Until now, little attention has been paid to finding ways to help treatment-resistant clients. There are a few full-length works (Collins 1969; Meloy et al. 1990; Rooney 1992; Harris and Watkins 1986) and many important, well-focused articles on counseling reluctant clients (for example, Dyer and Vriend 1973; Arcaya 1978; Berman and Segal

1982; Larke 1985). Nevertheless, because of the importance of the topic, the lack of material on the general problem of treatment resistance seems weak, and even less attention is devoted to gender differences in resistance.

During the last twenty years, problems such as battering, drug abuse, child abuse, and criminal behavior have received much attention, but with few exceptions, little comprehensive attention has been paid to the problem of working with involuntary and resistant clients. The literature has not adequately described resistance to counseling per se, nor has it shown how it is different from resistance to change. This work tackles these twin problems.

Whether the lack of attention to men's issues in the treatment of resistance is a form of sexism is a topic for another discussion, but it is beyond dispute that the problems of men, who occupy nearly 90 percent of the prison beds and a large percentage of addiction program slots in the country, are enormous. Young men, especially African-Americans, are the primary victims of violence in our culture, and it seems unlikely that our society will be able to solve other problems, such as domestic violence, unless we address the violence done to our young men as they grow into manhood.

Since 1986 many new developments have occurred in the field of counseling and psychotherapy, as well as in society. After the publication of *Counseling the Involuntary and Resistant Client* (1986) and *Tough Customers: Counseling Unwilling Clients* (1991), I have modified my views on some issues I narrated in these works. By providing an overview of these changes—cultural, personal, and professional—readers may find ways to improve their work with "new-age" clients.

First and foremost, research evidence is becoming clearer about what therapies work and how. There are fads in therapy, but the core ingredients of successful therapy are increasingly apparent. The terms "eclectic" and "integrative psychotherapy" describe attempts to think about common ingredients of successful therapy, and these core ingredients are explored here with respect to treatment-resistant clients.

Cognitive therapy also offers a language that may help counselors and therapists see common elements in all therapies. The present publication explores the implications of some cognitive-therapy principles for working with treatment-resistant clients. It also shows the overlap between several other psychodynamic theories and cognitive therapy.

Another important trend in psychotherapy is the rise of brief, solution-focused models. Counselors have developed brief therapies, which use a wide range of theories, from psychodynamic to cognitive-behavioral. The focus of each is on intense, short-term work. These models have particular importance for working with reluctant clients, who do not want to be in therapy at all, much less long-term therapy. Given a scarcity of time to work with most clients because of funding problems, brief approaches are necessary; though, I reject the notion that therapy should be done fast only because of funding limitations. After all, it would be absurd to write a book called *The One-Minute Neurosurgeon*; no one would want such surgery to be done quickly just to save money. Therapy takes whatever time it takes, but if we can find effective ways to do it faster, then fine. For a variety of reasons, the time limits of working with treatment-resistant clients must be considered.

My hope is that comments on these topics will contribute to the reader's personal as well as professional thinking. Readers looking for easy answers will be disappointed, of course, as will those looking for formulas. I welcome hearing from practitioners who have found successful methods to counsel their reluctant clients.

My interest in the resistant client began early in my graduate training, but I did not know it. I had been assigned to do psychological testing with a boy whose parents had called the university psychology department looking for help. The call was forwarded to my professor who saw an opportunity for a practicum student. When I arrived at the home of the boy, it quickly became obvious that he wanted no part of the testing his parents had arranged. He was uncooperative, though not physically defiant. Because of his poor verbal skills, he was probably not able to consciously form thoughts about what he was thinking and feeling about the experience. We muddled through the testing, but I did not think he had been fairly measured.

Back at the university, I asked my professor what I should have done. He answered, "Well, you just can't test some kids." This response left me puzzled because what is the point of testing (or counseling) if you cannot test people whose problems make them difficult subjects? In fact, many psychological tests are normed on a random sample from the population as a whole. But the norms do little good if the test is unusable with those clients at the edge of the bell curve.

Later, in graduate school in 1974, I enrolled in my first counseling practicum. During that time at the university, students in counseling programs first took a counseling theories class before they enrolled in the practicum. In the theories class students were required to be clients for advanced students enrolled in their practicums. This arrangement provided a steady supply of clients for practice. (Such requirements are now discouraged by the American Psychological Association accreditation program because it is considered unethical to coerce clients into treatment. More information on the ethics of involuntary counseling is covered later.)

In any event, my first client in the practicum informed me that she did not want to be counseled because she did not have any problems. This frustrated me. I did not know how to respond, and I insisted that we both had to do it because it was a requirement. My client became angry and wouldn't talk except to say, "Quit staring at me." Out of desperation, I suggested that the only way I could avoid staring at her was if we both sat back-to-back in our chairs so we could look away from each other. She agreed, and we sat this way for twenty minutes with the tension building. Finally, one of us laughed (probably in response to anxiety, but I don't remember whether it was hers or mine.) The tension broke, and we were able to turn around and talk about what we were going to do to get through our individual requirements.

Still later in graduate school, I was assigned to work with juvenile delinquents, who clearly did not want to be in counseling, and with many other clients who did not cooperate. Slowly, it dawned on me that counseling real people with real problems was not at all like what I had come to expect from reading textbooks. My professors did not seem to have suitable suggestions for dealing with the fact that many clients are not eager to be helped. This book provides some material for filling that gap.

While in graduate school, I took positions in vocational rehabilitation and corrections in Kansas City. Again, I experienced the problem of working with the resistant client. At the jail I was eventually promoted to an administrative position as training coordinator and immediately received anonymous hate mail from disgruntled corrections officers who resented that a "college kid" without experience as an officer would be chosen to direct the training program. Talk about resistance!

Leaving the jail, I took a position teaching corrections at

Washburn University in Topeka. Here, I learned that the students were only motivated by a desire to learn as much as they needed to get elective credits to apply to their degree requirements. After a few years of teaching, I yearned to work with people who wanted my services, so I decided to go into private practice. My first referral was a security guard who was arrested for indecent exposure in a pornographic movie theater. (He was arrested by an off-duty police officer whose whereabouts that evening apparently went unquestioned.) My client never admitted any offense and protested throughout counseling that he had never before been in an adult theater. So much for willing clients.

Gradually, it occurred to me that the problem of the involuntary and resistant client was big. It took me several years to name the problem (though I resist thinking of myself as a slow learner.) Now, when I think about this problem, it seems to be everywhere. However, it goes unrecognized and unmanaged by most therapists, who wistfully cling to the idea that most clients really want help and want to change.

My experience is that few people really want to be in counseling. Most adolescents are reluctant to be in counseling, and in marital therapy often either the husband or the wife has been dragged into treatment by the other. Both typically think the other person should do the changing! State-employed social workers see their share of resistance in child abuse and domestic violence cases. Of course, chemical dependency counselors deal with treatment-resistant clients. Most counseling approaches do not provide adequate guidance for ways to deal with the denial, projection of blame, and the externalization of responsibility that the treatment-resistant client shows.

**Most therapists deal with the treatment-resistant client, even though they may not want to!** The focus of this book is not exclusively on correctional counseling, though certainly correctional clients usually qualify as treatment resistant. Treatment-resistant clients include a special type of involuntary client, the client with the antisocial personality disorder.

Some therapists think of correctional clients as a discrete category of clients who are distinctly different from the type of clients with whom they wish to work. This is not the case. People in correctional programs are more similar to than different from other clients. Of course, many therapists in private practice receive referrals of present or former correctional clients. So, it is a mistake to focus too much on "correctional" counseling as though it were a distinct enterprise.

Ironically, in seminars I have given on counseling involuntary and resistant clients, invariably several people are present who would rather not be and who were required to attend because of continuing education requirements or because of the demands of administrators who wanted to get members of their staff better trained. Everywhere one looks there is evidence of coercion and of resistance to coercion. This reality changes everything in therapy if not also in education.

# Chapter 1

## *Implications of Involuntariness for Therapy*

$S$ean listened intently and felt a sense of relief when the judge deferred prosecution on the condition that he receive counseling. Not that he needed head shrinking, Sam thought, but the alternative was probably jail. Twelve sessions and I'm free, he mused. I can get through twelve sessions; no problem.

Sean's lawyer also thought the diversion program was a good deal. The counselor in the court services diversion program was only required to report to the judge that Sean had successfully completed the required session. So, with the lawyer's help, Sean arranged for his first appointment.

As the time for the first meeting approached, Sean began to feel angry at the whole mess. His wife still would not see him. He had left messages for her at the battered women's shelter, but she never returned his calls. He was sure the staff were not giving her the messages; they were busybodies interfering where they did not belong. If they had kept their noses out of it, he would not have been dragged out of his own house like a criminal.

Whose business was it, he thought, if he and his wife had a fight? What right did anyone have to tell him what he could and could not do in his own home? Besides, the two of them could have worked it out themselves if they had been left alone. Anyway, she had provoked him and goaded him until he could not stand it anymore  Now, he was paying the price. As angry as he was at her, he knew that he wanted her back, and he sometimes felt depressed and angry enough to kill himself—and her—if she would not cooperate.

Sean arrived for his initial counseling session just on time. He had to rush to get there because he was on his lunch hour. He almost lost his job when he was arrested and detained, and he could not afford any more time off. He barely had time to get seated in the waiting room when a man about the age of his younger brother called his name.

"Hi, I'm Jeff. Grab a cup of coffee and come on in."

Sean and Jeff walked down the hall to a small, tile-floored room with a couple of easy chairs and a few sick-looking plants. Jeff motioned to a chair and asked Sean to have a seat.

"Sean, I know a little about your situation from the court record and imagine you're less than thrilled about having to come here, even though you chose this over prosecution. Is that right?"

"Yes," Sean responded cautiously. He had figured that this counselor was going to start by lecturing him for a while about wife beating, so the beginning was a bit of a surprise. It took a little wind out of his sails. Jeff then asked Sean to talk a little about what he wanted to accomplish in counseling, a request that also took Sean off guard.

"Frankly," Sean told Jeff, he didn't know of anything he needed to accomplish, except to get his wife back.

"I see," Jeff said. "You mean there's nothing about yourself you really need to change? You're a perfect human being caught in an unfair situation?"

Sean started to become a little hot under the collar. Who was this sarcastic jerk anyway? "I never said I was perfect," he replied. "But what I need, you can't give me unless you can talk my wife into letting me come home."

"I wouldn't if I could," Jeff said. "Anyway, I imagine she'd tell me you have to change first."

"Change what?" Sean asked angrily.

"Listen, Sean, please don't be mad at me. I didn't file the charges against you, and I didn't order you here. I just want to know if there was anything you want to talk about while you're in counseling."

"What good will it do to come in here and yak about it? That's not going to get my wife back," Sean retorted. He was still angry, but he also recognized that blaming the counselor would be unreasonable.

"You don't think there's anything you might learn that would help you get along better with your wife? If so, you're a rare person; almost everybody could use a little on that score," Jeff said.

"Sure, I'm human. I just don't think I'm the only one at fault in this deal. She ought to be in counseling too, if getting along better is what we're trying to do."

"I didn't say you were the only one at fault," Jeff answered. "I didn't say anyone was at fault. Maybe your wife should be here, but she's not. So, the question is, do you want to see if there's anything you and I can do in the next twelve weeks to help you get along better with her? I can't guarantee we'll find anything, and if we do, I can't guarantee she'll let you move home. But, that's all we can do. You want to try?"

"I guess so," Sean said, weary and depressed.

Jeff knew Sean wasn't going to be an easy client. He realized that Sean had not chosen counseling freely. Sean was a typical reluctant client who did not perceive his responsibility for his plight. He blamed others for it. Jeff knew that he could not counsel him until Sean admitted his responsibility, but he also knew he needed to help Sean see a value in counseling. Jeff also knew that talking about blame on anyone's part is usually futile.

Jeff also realized that Sean, like most people, would dislike being told what to do. Everyone prefers to feel that choices exist, and we resent those who restrict our choices. Therefore, Jeff explicitly disassociated himself from the coercion behind Sean's being there. He did so without criticizing the judge, the police, or Sean's wife. Jeff knew that Sean would rebel against him if he were linked with the court order.

Sean also made it clear to Jeff that he doubted whether talk would do much good. Jeff knew that people who felt this way seldom ask for counseling, which, after all, is just talk. He knew there was no way to prove the worth of counseling to Sean, who would gain faith in the counseling process only through success with it. Minimally, Jeff wanted to elicit Sean's cooperation to begin, because it was Sean's only hope.

Sean had not elected counseling, and this situation created many roadblocks to getting started. Jeff also knew that even when these roadblocks were overcome, Sean would still resist changing. The form his resistance would take could only be imagined at this first session. Would he feel less of a man if he could not dominate his wife? Did he feel the need to control people in general, and would he resist giving up the advantages of that way of living for the advantages of more equal, reciprocal relationships? Would his wife find the changes in him satisfying and sufficient enough to warrant a new start, and would she talk to him without blaming him exclusively for their past relationship problems?

Each person and each couple is different. Even people who ask for help resist it, and Jeff knew that people who are forced into counseling pose special obstacles, as well as unique and fascinating challenges. Jeff realized that if he had any hope of helping Sean, he would need to process the full range of his understanding of change and resistance to change. Jeff would need to understand the special agony of the person who is floundering in deep water but fights off the lifeguard who is trying to help.

## Societal Changes

Society itself has changed. Addiction is a continuing but worsening problem that should be considered when counseling treatment-resistant clients. Drug and alcohol abuse remain a problem. Gangs, fueled with drug money, have become more prevalent, even in smaller cities. Counseling gang members requires a knowledge of gangs and the role they play in the life of their members. Related to these social problems is the sickening rate of violence and death, especially among young black males, who, if they survive, often become involuntary clients in counseling programs in corrections and other social agencies.

No counseling technique can overcome the impact of this high level of violence on young people and others. Counseling is important, but other social and economic programs are crucial for the solutions to these social problems. Counselors can play a significant role in helping clients discover and access ways to thwart these issues to create a better life for themselves and those around them. This book, however, is intended as an aid to counselors struggling with difficult clients, to help them discover what works best. And, if it helps just a little, this is positive, but counselors' expectations of what counseling can do must be tempered by realism.

## Definition of Therapy

A simplified definition of therapy is a relationship in which one person comes to another with a problem and requests help. The treatment-resistant, help-rejecting client, like Sean, does not seek help and may not consciously accept or admit that he has a problem.

What does the therapist do when the patient does not identify a problem? Is it the therapist's job to provide treatment anyway? Should the therapist convince the client that counseling is needed? Should the therapist refuse to do counseling until the client requests it? If the latter were the case, there would be little for correctional counselors to do. Therapists would rarely treat juveniles, who seldom want to come for counseling. In Sean's case, would it be practical to insist that he quickly make a clear statement that indicated he recognized and desired therapy? Rather, is it the therapist's job to guide Sean and other clients into such a recognition during the course of therapy?

Most teaching about psychotherapy assumes a voluntary relationship between the client and the counselor. This assumption seems basic in most academic teaching texts about counseling. This is so, despite the obvious fact that many clients are coerced. Nugent (1994), in a discussion of counseling therapy and ethics, described an exception to counseling being voluntary when the counselor believes that harm is clear and imminent. Nevertheless, even this allowance rules out counseling for a vast array of clients who are referred for treatment. We recognize resistance to change, but resistance to counseling is not appreciated. Many clients, like Sean, do not really know what counseling is. Therefore, they do not know what it can do for them. They resist counseling outright based on false impressions and stereotypes about therapy taken from the media and perhaps from minimal contacts with other professionals who they have confused with therapists, such as probation officers or other government officials.

This failure to recognize the special problem of resistance to counseling is especially troublesome since many therapists take their first jobs in agencies with difficult clients, such as prisons or state hospitals. Even geriatric counselors face resistant clients (Robison et al. 1989). Only after gaining some experience with these resistant clients do most therapists move into private practices or other work where the clients are more likely to have chosen to come for counseling.

Many therapists, including writers about therapy, are in denial about the nature of their work. We do not want to admit that clients reject us and what we do. How do we respond if we cannot recognize that clients are rejecting the very concept of psychotherapy, perhaps for good reasons? Can we be objective and therapeutic if we do not understand why clients might reject the notion of psychotherapy? Can we understand why a client rejects therapy without first beginning therapy?

Nevertheless, it is incorrect to assume that voluntary clients readily identify and talk about their problems. Few patients can label their problem, much less express their issues to the therapist in the first session. Many clients who seek therapy are not able to verbalize their problems. Often, they are quite poor at labeling their symptoms. Even in physical medicine, patients may not know the reason for their distress. The cause of a broken bone is usually easy to identify as is "the problem" (the broken bone) and the symptoms (pain and inability to use the limb), but other ailments, such as cancer or viruses, require diagnosis.

With involuntary clients, their ability to discuss and label their problem is confounded by their anger at being coerced into treatment. These emotions mask other feelings, which, if recognized, would lead them to make better problem statements. If Sean, for example, could defuse his anger at being forced into treatment, he might be able to express the powerlessness and shame that he feels. He might be able to see "the problem" in a different way.

Further complicating the issue of helping clients to talk about problems is the reality that an identified problem may not have a clear cause or causes. Many patients are unaware of the symptoms of illness, and some symptoms may be incorrectly associated or linked with the wrong causes or problems. In addition, due to the many theories or explanations of behavior, counselors need to state their theoretical orientation (such as Alderian, family therapy, or others) when they describe the presenting problem. A therapist trained in one school of thought may view a client's problems differently than another therapist who has received another type of training. In the case of Sean, depending on your orientation, you might identify the causes of Sean's spouse abuse based on any of the following theories:

- his aggressive personality
- a violent society
- ineffective communication skills
- a provocative spouse
- bad parental role models
- misuse of alcohol
- too much testosterone
- environmental stressors
- an evil streak

Sean may have difficulty discussing his situation because it is so complex. Counselors may have similar problems because of their varied theoretical backgrounds.

The issue of identifying problems, causes, and symptoms becomes more significant for those who work with involuntary clients. Involuntary clients often angrily point fingers and identify the problem as external to themselves. For example, the drug seller may see his problem as a law that is outdated, while a therapist may see the problem as irresponsible thinking. Or, a white-collar offender (Harris 1991) may see the problem as a mere technical violation of trading rules, while a therapist may not even understand on what basis the person was convicted.

Therapy typically operates from the position that the individual must take personal responsibility. He must own his actions and feelings. This requires that he rejects externalization of responsibility, something the involuntary client often has difficulty doing. This means that from the beginning of therapy with the involuntary client, the therapist's and the client's worldviews are in conflict. This conflict often leads to the therapist concluding that the client is *unwilling* to assume responsibility, while the client feels *unable* to do so. When the client rejects the therapy and the therapist, the therapy process is tense and filled with conflict from the beginning of the time together.

The therapist may interpret the client's rejection of responsibility as anything from unconscious denial to lying. Of course, how the therapist looks at the client's behavior has an impact on the interventions the therapist chooses. When the client's (mis)behavior is seen as willful and conscious, therapists (along with the rest of society) often believe that punishment or some type of negative consequence is an appropriate response. We choose the stick over the carrot. However, if the therapist sees the client's behavior as unconsciously motivated or externally caused, then the therapist is apt to choose softer, more "therapeutic" responses.

Under the guise of therapy, some treatment programs may become excuses for delivering punishment to clients who "choose" to reject personal responsibility. Behavior modification programs, for example, can become good vehicles for the delivery of punishment to clients whose views of responsibility do not match the therapist's. If the client does not behave appropriately, he is punished. If he responds angrily to the punishment, he is punished again. All this contradicts the assumption of learning theory that behavior is not chosen but rather shaped by the environmental contingencies.

Clearly, it is important for therapists to be aware of their own assumptions about human behavior and to be aware of their theories of treatment. Without such awareness, therapists may easily rationalize treatment as punishment. They may be excessively confrontational not to help the client but to blame him. Finally, they may use ineffective interventions based on blind faith in their efficacy. Treatment programs should have internally consistent assumptions, and interventions should be rationally based on theory and available research. If this is done, the results of treatment can be monitored and improved.

## Importance of the Theoretical Frame of Reference

How do counselors' theories of counseling affect their basic approaches to working with treatment-resistant clients? Joseph Weiss (1994), in an interesting psychodynamically based model, proposes that patients are always attempting to disconfirm false and dysfunctional (pathogenic) beliefs that they acquired in early childhood. In therapy, the patient responds to the therapist as a parent or treats the therapist as the patient was treated by his parent. In either case, Weiss believes that patients are looking for information to refute those beliefs that distort their healthy interactions with others.

Assume for a moment that a patient had parents who were excessively controlling. In therapy, such a patient might test the counselor to see whether the therapist will try to be controlling, as well. Therapists who respond with clear consequences to missed appointments, for example, may confirm to patients that they will be victims under the therapist's power. On the other hand, the patient may attempt to control the therapist (and therapy) as he (the client) was controlled as a child. For example, the client may choose topics that the therapist considers unimportant or inappropriate and avoid the issues that the therapist perceives as crucial.

If the therapist responds to such efforts by controlling the session, the client may conclude from his test that he was right that other people will try to control him without regard to his feelings. In Weiss' model, the therapist might be advised to show the client that his attempts to control the therapy were not harmful to the therapist and that the therapist was not angry with the attempts. With this insight, the client would feel safe from being controlled and attacked. He would be free then to give up his belief that others are always out to control him, and he would be free to give up his own controlling, testing behavior. Nevertheless, the counselor needs to be aware of the cultural context of the client that may influence his lack of comfort and his belief in the credibility of the counseling process. Some individuals, due to their unique cultural perspective, may not respond well to traditional forms of counseling.

However, let us now make different assumptions. Instead of assuming that people are trying to disconfirm their basic pathogenic beliefs in therapy and are setting up tests to do so, assume that clients are merely acting on their dysfunctional beliefs. Thus, a client who tries to dictate the topics of therapy might be acting on the belief that he should not have the limits that others do, that he is special in a narcissistic sense. In this case, the therapist who does not respond with clear structure may be permitting the client to retain a dysfunctional view that, in fact, needs to be challenged. Thus, whatever the therapist's or counselor's theory of therapy, it is of crucial importance to recognize its role in planning interventions.

Some theories of therapy may overlap and may be integrated into a common theory (see Regazio-Digilio and Ivey [1993] for an attempt to integrate counseling theory into a developmental model); however, contradictory theoretical premises may make integration impossible. This text does not claim to have resolved all the inconsistencies. Rather, the author hopes that by describing a variety of approaches to the treatment-resistant client, readers will choose what makes sense to them and is appropriate for each particular client.

## Similarities in Theory

Weiss' psychodynamic theory has remarkable similarities with other approaches, including cognitive therapy. Weiss theorized that children form their beliefs from early childhood experiences. This is similar to cognitive schema theory (Young 1990). Yet, Weiss' theory generates numerous new ideas for working with the treatment-resistant client. For example, if Weiss is correct that people wish to have their false beliefs disconfirmed, then the client who is refusing treatment may be wishing that someone (such as the therapist) will firmly insist on therapy. Under this framework, the client who rejects therapy is saying that he does not feel worthy of attention or capable of change. And when therapists dismiss such a client as "unmotivated" for treatment, they confirm the client's conclusions about himself (Larrabee 1982).

Therapists may misinterpret badly the resistance to entering treatment many clients display (Heitler 1976; Hartman 1979). At a minimum, such resistance is a statement from the client about his life experience. The rejection of treatment may be a test clients make hoping that they will be able to disprove those beliefs that they know to be harmful (Weiss 1994). Thus, clients who say they do not want treatment, in fact, want it very much.

Solution-focused psychotherapies offer another example of the importance of understanding one's theoretical frame of reference for working with treatment-resistant clients. In solution-focused psychotherapies, the therapist attempts to identify the outcomes a client would like as a result of counseling (Selekman 1993). Such a focus on outcomes does not require client and counselor to agree on or even to identify perceived problems or causes of problems. For example, in marital therapy a couple may agree that they would like to be able to spend time together each evening quietly eating dinner, but they may have widely divergent views about what has been keeping them from doing this. A correctional client may agree that staying out of legal trouble is a good objective but might argue over the reasons he got into trouble in the first place.

Focusing on solutions may be one way to help clients overcome their resistance to therapy. Such an approach gets around the placing of responsibility (blame), which the client rejects. Yet, even in a solution-focused approach, the client must be reasonably willing to cooperate with the therapeutic process and, probably at some level, must be committed to making some changes.

In the absence of at least a superficial level of cooperation, the therapist must focus on understanding the client's basic resistance to entering treatment and must find a way to work toward getting a treatment contract, either formally or informally. The formation of the treatment contract becomes the essence of the work with the treatment-resistant client. The treatment contract is an understanding, either verbal or written, of the goals and purposes of the counseling. By having such a contract, clients will be able to work toward goals they see as important and worthwhile.

In a recent book on using cognitive therapy for dealing with substance abuse (Beck et al. 1994), the authors emphasized that a collaborative relationship was the essence of cognitive therapy. Mere application of techniques would be useless without attention to building a therapeutic relationship. The authors also emphasized the importance of setting an agenda for each cognitive therapy session.

Other authors propose a model for gauging the client's stage of therapy and the client's accessibility for intervention. Prochaska and Diclimente (1992) suggest that people go through five stages in seeking help:

- precontemplation
- contemplation
- preparation
- action
- maintenance

In the stage of precontemplation, people have not considered the need for change. Therefore, they are resistant to seeking and entering treatment. In the contemplative stage, they are thinking about but not doing anything about their problems, but they are a little closer to accepting help. In the preparation stage, they are beginning to gather information and insights about what they need to do. At this stage they recognize the need for counseling assistance. In the action stage, they are actively implementing change and using therapy to get ideas and suggestions. Then, in the maintenance phase, they consolidate the changes they have made. Interventions depend on the current stage of the client.

For example, with precontemplative clients, the counselor's role is to help build the client's awareness, while clients at the action stage may be amenable to behavioral methods such as homework assignments. Though this theory of stages of client's receptivity to therapy is helpful, it does not provide detailed suggestions for how to move clients from a precontemplative to a contemplative stage or higher. Most psychotherapies, at least as commonly construed, are applicable to clients who are at least in the contemplative stage.

By contrast, this volume explores the problems posed by the precontemplative client. These clients do not seek a change process because they do not perceive a need to change. They also may avoid consideration of change because they fear and misperceive both the change process and therapy. Once the therapist or counselor helps clients commit to counseling, clients may still resist change. Most therapists understand resistance to change, because almost every major psychotherapy theory considers it, but most therapists do not understand resistance to therapy itself.

Many psychotherapeutic relationships are not truly voluntary. Many clients would rather be elsewhere since they do not see themselves as responsible for the problem. Even clients who seek treatment to alleviate anxiety or emotional distress are, as Haley (1963, 1983) noted, essentially coerced into treatment by the pain. However, clients who have externalized responsibility for their problem are not ready to consent to therapy designed to change them. After all, they do not acknowledge anything they need to change. (Note: Weiss' psychodynamic theory proposes that unconsciously clients do want to change their false or pathogenic beliefs.)

Consider the first session with a reluctant client as a sales call. Menninger (1958) in his work on psychoanalytic technique explained that analysts were selling responsibility while patients were seeking to purchase relief from pain. Few clients would agree to make the purchase if they knew they would be expected to work hard and stop blaming others for their problems, which is the general goal of therapy.

To persuade clients to participate in therapy they must be convinced that they will receive some benefit from their participation. To a highly anxious client, the hoped-for benefit may be relief from discomfort. On the other hand, angry clients may hope that their enemies get their "just deserts," hardly a goal most counselors would agree to help achieve.

Finding a goal or benefit for counseling for the reluctant client is often a highly creative search and may represent the most important part of the work because it identifies the client's motivation. In traditional psychotherapy, the counselor more or less expects the client to come in with goals, or at least problems, in mind and with motivation to solve those problems. Those that do this are the easy clients who are already at the contemplative stage of development. Many, perhaps most, clients lack insight into the causes of their symptoms. The existence of symptoms of distress commonly brought to therapy (such as sleeplessness and irritability) suggest that clients experience some internal conflict for which they may have no conscious explanation. The client has not begun to fully "contemplate" the issues. When the counselor helps the client develop the treatment contract, this is an attempt to move troublesome issues up the client's ladder of awareness to a more conscious level, which helps the client to take responsibility for his problems.

Another example demonstrates the process of helping clients identify outcomes and benefits for which they are willing to work. Batterers typically blame their spouses for provoking them. They insist that everything will be fine if others will just stay out of their business. A traditional approach to the batterer might be to insist that he acknowledge his violence and stop denying that he has a problem controlling it. Such an approach may be logical, but, typically, it meets with a great deal of resistance. The batterer may be re-enacting with his spouse what his parents did with him, and if the therapist attempts to exert power over the client, the client will engage in a power struggle to avoid being defeated.

An alternative approach might be to help the client identify what he will need to do to convince his wife to reconcile. This alternative approach need not place the counselor in a confrontational position to the client because the counselor does not need to draw any judgments about the fairness of the wife's requirements for reconciliation. Rather, the counselor is merely exploring the reality of how the client can meet his needs.

As the counseling progresses, the counselor needs to be respectful of the client's conscious and unconscious goals, but the counselor does not need to cooperate with objectionable goals. For example, if the batterer states that he wants his wife to obey him, there is no reason to try to help the client achieve this. Depending on one's theory, the counselor could offer a variety of responses. Those counselors using reality therapy could ask how such a demand would help the client feel love and belonging (Glasser 1965). Counselors employing cognitive therapy could inquire about the advantages and disadvantages of the demand. However, the therapist employing psychodynamic theory could view the statement of the demand as a test to see how the therapist will respond.

## Confrontation

Many counselors are unable to work with the reluctant client because they insist that the client "own" a problem--in terms that the counselor can accept. Many chemical dependency counselors, for example, insist that the client quit "denying" his alcoholism and accept the alcoholic label. Similarly, many batterers are told that they must acknowledge their violence.

Yet, what good does it do to confront these issues this way if the client hunkers down and refuses to talk, or worse, just does not return for another session? The counselor arrogantly can claim that the client was not motivated for counseling or change, but isn't it just as logical to say that the counselor was graceless and clumsy?

Throughout this book, the author emphasizes the need to understand all clients and their particular motivations and respect the client's right to decide not to change. Most psychotherapy models, when closely examined, consistently emphasize nonconfrontational, nonadversarial methods (Otani 1989). Similarly, research consistently reveals that confrontation tends to arouse defenses and make clients more resistant (Miller 1985).

There is a time and a place for head-to-head confrontation (Forest 1982). This emphasis on understanding clients does not mean that confrontation is never useful. Confrontation by peers or family members may be accepted and heard by clients because of the depth of their relationship with each other. Counselors in institutions or hospitals who have captive clients for a limited time may be able to force effective examination of issues by use of aggressive confrontation. Nevertheless, most such confrontations fail in the long term because a truly resistant client can defeat the best counselor.

The relationship between counselor and client is fragile and easily threatened. It is much more likely that clients will reveal themselves when they feel it is safe to do so than when they feel pressured. Consequently, in most cases, it is more productive to try to create a safe environment rather than one of confrontation.

Traditionally, one method of dealing with resistance is to confront it by pointing out how it manifests itself. Then, the resistance is clarified by examining what motivates it. Next, its deep roots are interpreted. Finally, the process of working through it occurs over the course of therapy by repetition of the confrontation, clarification, and interpretation (Strean 1985). Of course, there also are other views on how to confront resistance in counseling.

It is necessary for counselors not to compromise themselves, but perhaps it is not important to establish control through confrontation. Counselors can quietly act on their own values without implying to others that their values are wrong. Most importantly, counselors need not articulate their view to the client that he needs therapy. The realization of this is the client's ultimate responsibility. Most people reject being told that they are sick or wrong. Thus, announcing it serves little purpose and may impede clients from confronting their deficiencies honestly.

Premature confrontation of such clients may result not in self-examination but in development of a symmetrical, escalating struggle for control between the counselor and the client. Mental health center records are filled with charts of clients who come once and depart angrily, with the counselor's notes suggesting that the client was not amenable to counseling (Varga 1971; West 1975; Kloss and Karan 1979; Epperson et al. 1983).

The issue of whether and how to confront resistance is difficult to settle. The only thing that is clear is that counselors should not confront to ventilate and make themselves feel better or to satisfy their own needs. Ellis (1985; Ellis et al. 1988), typically known for forcefully disputing irrational beliefs through logic and persuasion, commented that when clients resist because they doubt your point, the counselor should argue expertly with them. When they resist because they do not like therapy in general, it is important to be personable and to build the relationship.

Ellis also acknowledged that some confrontation styles are indirect and easy going, while other styles are direct and hard nosed. Cognitive therapists prefer indirect, Socratic questioning, which is less confrontational than the rational emotive therapist's direct argumentation. The indirect method couples empathic reflection with questioning to lead to a point rather than direct disagreements and challenges to make a point. For example, the counselor might say, "What did that behavior get for you?" rather than, "Your action only succeeded in making your predicament worse; apparently, you persist in believing you shouldn't have to work hard at finding the solution for this problem."

Confrontation is often used with alcoholics to break down denial, but research points to the destructive impact that counselor hostility has on therapy. The client perceives this hostility during confrontation. Too much confrontation seems to arouse anxiety and also triggers self-defense rather than coping and problem-solving behaviors. Feedback about the discrepancy between actual and ideal self could be used in confrontation if it were coupled with feedback about improvement (Miller 1985). This may occur when the counseling process develops attainable and specific goals for the client to try to meet.

Thus, counselors see low motivation as a client characteristic. However, a more useful view is to see motivation as a complex interaction of factors, including characteristics of the therapist. Miller also pointed out that verbalized resistance to participating in counseling has little empirical correlation with actual participation in counseling or with treatment outcome. Counselors usually define the motivated client as one who is distressed, accepts the therapist's point of view, and complies. Ellis has noted that sometimes a client quite correctly and rationally decides the counselor is off the mark with a particular interpretation or cannot help for other reasons and, therefore, rationally resists.

Another therapist (Bratter 1974) offers a compelling account of the development of his personal style with addicts. He strongly argued for the need for intense involvement with and confrontation of "unmotivated" clients. Like Ellis, he seems to have the ability to confront without appearing not to care, and as long as clients perceive the caring, they probably will not react as intensely with denial or other forms of resistance. (It is quite possible that addicts in Bratter's case and New Yorkers in Ellis' case can tolerate confrontation better than small-town or rural clients.) Forrest (1982) offers a thoughtful discussion of confrontation with the alcoholic whose denial impedes progress. However, research on this subject is sparse.

Erickson (1980) demonstrates another approach to dealing with the resistant, abrasive client. While his skills are probably beyond replication by most, nevertheless, his policy clearly was to meet patients' needs but on terms they proposed. He believed the therapist must develop a keen sensitivity to patients' inner processes so that they can meet their problems by use of already acquired learning. Though, at times, Erickson may have appeared to be as abrasive as his patients, he was never adversarial. He viewed the patient's attack as a symptom whose power could be used by the therapist to help the patient.

Until there is more research on confrontation techniques, the following suggestions may prove useful: First, the counselor should assess the client's capacity to form a relationship and to bond with the counselor. Clients who can form a therapeutic alliance through empathy should be helped to do so. Some clients may not form this alliance unless the counselor brings the issue into the open by talking about the client's inability to trust or relate. Other clients (antisocial personalities) may lack the capacity to form relationships, so counseling cannot proceed with relationship building as a foundation. The counselor may need to focus initially on setting structure and providing incentive for behavior change or compliance with program requirements. However, much of the work with antisocial clients involves explicating thinking errors and highlighting the clients' choice to be responsible (see chapter 7 on counseling antisocial clients.)

Second, when the relationship is reasonably secure, and some confrontation is required, the relationship should be able to withstand indirect questioning about beliefs that underlie resistance to counseling. They might include the client's belief that, "I shouldn't be forced into treatment; I don't have a problem," or "Counseling can't help my kind of problem." If these low-key measures do not work, the counselor can always use a more vigorous, forceful challenge to the client's resistance to counseling.

Third, when the reluctant client engages in a counseling process, other resistances to change will appear as with any client. The counselor will have to decide how to deal with that resistance. The choices are many: looking for and disputing irrational beliefs, exploring feelings associated with the resistance, and using paradox and other techniques recommended by various counseling approaches.

## Resistance to Initiating Therapy: A Case in Point

Contrasting styles of meeting resistance may become clearer by examining one client's case and alternative approaches to it. Basch (1982) presented a condensed account of the initial interview of a case and a succinct summary of his feeling about the dialog. He noted that other therapists might have handled the situation differently, but just as effectively. Basch also commented, the most frustrating case is one in which the client resists examining the resistance and gets into an interpersonal struggle with the counselor.

The person in the case reported was clearly resistant. Though the client sought out the therapist, it was not for therapy but for advice about what do to about his children. Thus, he in no way accepted responsibility for his difficulties and bridled when the therapist suggested he had some problems.

The patient, Mr. Adam Hoheit, is a forty-five-year-old investment banker. His bearing and appearance radiate success and authority. The following is a condensed account of the first interview.

**Therapist:**   (walking into the waiting room and offering his hand) Mr. Hoheit? I am Dr. Basch.

Mr. Hoheit:   (indifferently shaking the proffered hand) I have to be out of here by 2:00, and you are five minutes late, doctor.

**Therapist:**    Come in please.

Mr. Hoheit:   (settling down in the designated chair) Will we be done by 2:00, doctor? I have a meeting by 2:15.

**Therapist:** Will we be done with what?

**Mr. Hoheit:** Right, I guess you don't even know what I'm here for. Actually, it shouldn't take too long. Abner Tatum was your patient, and he is my client. We were talking at lunch the other day, and I mentioned my problem to him. Abner said he wanted to stay out of it, but he said you had been of great help to him during his divorce, so I thought perhaps I could use some of your counsel in my circumstances, too.

**Therapist:** I'd be glad to be of help if I can.

**Mr. Hoheit:** It's not really for me. I need advice regarding my chidren. I want to know whether, in your professional opinion, my getting a divorce from my wife will hurt them. I have a boy age five, and two daughters, sixteen and fourteen. The two older ones will be leaving home to go to college fairly soon anyway, but the five-year-old worries me a little.

**Therapist:** I don't think that's a question I can answer. If you'll tell me about your situation, I may be able to clarify your thinking.

**Mr. Hoheit:** You mean if I can give you more information about him then you can tell me how my boy will be affected? I suppose it does differ with each personality.

**Therapist:** No. I would like to hear from you about your children, their personalities, and the effects you think a divorce will have on them because that will help me get a better picture of what's going on with you.

**Mr. Hoheit:** All this will take a long time. I have to be out of here by 2:00 you know.

**Therapist:** There is no telling how long it will take. If there is reason to meet more than once, I'm prepared to do so.

**Mr. Hoheit:** (with a sneer on his face and a sarcastic tone) Sounds to me like you're trying to set up something for yourself, doctor.

**Therapist:** Please explain yourself.

**Mr. Hoheit:** Well, I asked you a simple question. I came to get a professional opinion from you as I would from a dentist, a lawyer, or a surgeon. I'm perfectly willing to pay what it costs to get it, but you are already making

|              | me into a client or a patient—whatever you people call it—and I'm just telling you before we go any further that I just might not care for that idea. What do you say to that? |
|--------------|---|
| Therapist:   | First of all, the question you asked me is not, as you suggest, a simple one. Moreover, as I told you, it is impossible to answer it as you asked it. I am willing to believe that you didn't know that, and I could understand your disappointment at being told that it was so. However, what I'd like you to explain is the tone of your voice and the look on your face when you said I was "trying to set something up" for myself. It sounded cynical and sarcastic, as if there was something dirty going on here. It seemed to me as if your initial purpose in coming here was forgotten, and your goal was not to enlist my help but to make me feel guilty and ashamed. For some reason you felt a need to attack me. |
| Mr. Hoheit:  | (silence) |
| Therapist:   | Well? |
| Mr. Hoheit:  | You and my wife. |
| Therapist:   | Hmm. |
| Mr. Hoheit:  | That's what she complains about. (in a falsetto voice) "You're attacking me. You're continually undermining me. I love you, but if I am going to retain my sanity, I have to leave you, Adam." Silly damned nonsense. |
| Therapist:   | You mean it's your wife who is leaving you? I was under the impression that you were going to seek a divorce. |
| Mr. Hoheit:  | What's the difference who is leaving whom! It's the boy I'm concerned about. |
| Therapist:   | It sounds to me as if you are in a lot of trouble with yourself and that we have much more to talk about. It's getting close to the time you said you had to leave. I would suggest that we make at least two more appointments so that I may clarify your situation for myself and make my recommendations. |
| Mr. Hoheit:  | So you think I need therapy? |
| Therapist:   | There's very little doubt in my mind about that. The |

<table>
<tr><td></td><td>question is whether or not you can lend yourself to that process and, if so, what form it should take.</td></tr>
</table>

Mr. Hoheit: question is whether or not you can lend yourself to that process and, if so, what form it should take.

Mr. Hoheit: Listen, the people I'm supposed to meet with aren't that important. I can tell them to wait if you have the time to go on.

Therapist: I did have more time allotted for this first meeting, but I wouldn't feel comfortable going on knowing that I was willfully inconveniencing the people waiting for you. How long will your meeting take?

Mr. Hoheit: An hour, maybe an hour and a half. Definitely no more.

Therapist: If you have the time, I could see you later in the day.

Mr. Hoheit: I don't want to keep you.

Therapist: It's no problem. I have to stay late anyway today. Would 5:30 be okay?

Mr. Hoheit: Fine, thank you, doctor.

Therapist: You're welcome. Good-bye till then, Mr. Hoheit.

This patient displays a narcissistic sense of entitlement. He feels perfectly justified in demanding that the world meet his needs to the exclusion of all other reality. Incensed that he was kept waiting for a few minutes, he has no hesitation about inconveniencing others when he feels it is in his interest to do so. It would, of course, have been a serious mistake to indulge him in this attitude. As it turned out, Mr. Hoheit did come back. Psychotherapy was recommended, and he was seen three times a week for a period of several months. He was able to gain sufficient insight into his behavior to ease the strain between himself and his wife considerably. According to Basch (1982):

> His need to control everyone and everything around him was rooted in his fear that if he did not do so he would be seen as weak, gullible, and easily imposed on; similar to the way in which he experienced his father. None of this was, of course, evident or suspected when I first met Mr. Hoheit. I bring up this material to illustrate an extreme example of a not uncommon situation in which the patient's fear that the therapist will not be strong enough to withstand the onslaught of the patient's needs leads him to wrestle the therapist

from the very first meeting or telephone call for control of the therapeutic situation, hoping against hope all the while that the doctor will not be intimidated. Since at that point therapy has not yet begun, there is no basis for dealing with the potential patient's behavior by interpretation. Attempts to placate the patient are seen by him as weakness on the part of the therapist and may well frighten him into finding some pretext for not returning.

It was most instructive for me to see that after the first few encounters with this patient, in which I apparently proved to him that I had the requisite strength to deal with him, the resistance to treatment dissipated and did not present a problem in the years we subsequently worked together. There was, of course, the expected intrapsychic resistance to uncovering aspects of repressed and disavowed memories, feelings and motives, but it was clear to both of us that the struggle was within him and not with me.

There are many different ways in which patients who need to do so attempt to dominate the therapist. Mr. Hoheit is presented only as a dramatic illustration of what often confronts us in a more subtle and disguised way. Nor am I advocating my approach to this particular patient as paradigmatic. Another therapist might have handled the situation differently but equally effectively. This particular clinical example is only given to illustrate that when a patient's resistance takes the form of acting out the question "Who is in control here?" it behooves the therapist to respond, in whatever way is congenial to his personality, "I am" (Basch 1982).

An important disagreement with Basch's approach stems from the question of who should be in control in counseling: the counselor or the client. Basch answers: the counselor. A different view is that the counselor should be in charge of himself or herself while not challenging the client's autonomy, either. That is, each person should be in charge only of himself or herself.

Basch was correct in not allowing himself to be manipulated into extending the session, an extension which he knew would have inconvenienced others. However, was it unnecessarily antagonistic to confront Mr. Hoheit by telling him that his tone of voice was cynical, sarcastic, and attacking? Although this may have been true, many clients might become more defensive and angry when they are confronted in this way.

Basch's view that the client is revealing fears about being controlled is similar to Weiss' notion that clients are seeking to have their dysfunctional beliefs proven wrong. The issue is how to respond to clients and whether to confront clients quickly and forcefully. The counselor must decide each case individually.

# Chapter 2

# The Three C's of Counseling Reluctant Clients

## Resistance: Definition Depends on Theory

Some writers criticize the concept of resistance as outmoded and counterproductive. Anderson and Stewart (1983), for example, described resistance facetiously as the client doing things the counselor does not like. Other authors point to the inherent difficulty in defining the term "resistance" without reference to a specific psychological theory. Driscoll defined resistance: "Resistance indicates opposition to something with clear intent or purpose to oppose." Messer (1992) examined Driscoll's supposedly theory-neutral definition of resistance and analyzed how theory bound it was. Messer replied, "This definition is couched in the language of intention, which is a mental or cognitive construct that classical behaviorists would oppose (resist?). It also implies a conscious attitude, thereby not readily encompassing a theory of unconscious motivation; language definition and theory are inextricably intertwined, and the effort to disentangle them typically leads to impoverished definitions and concepts."

In addition to the dependence of the definition of resistance on theory, the term resistance seems to carry a negative tone that is unfortunate. Ansbacher (1982) said that resistance to change represents at least a degree of stability and integration of personality. Consequently, it is a mistake to think all resistance is negative. People construct a worldview that works for them to greater and lesser degrees, and it would be dysfunctional to abandon one's worldview too easily because then the world would be chaotic and unpredictable.

## Resistance as Seen in Various Schools of Therapy

Most models of therapy and theories of personality offer some definition of resistance to change and attempt to locate the source of the resistance. Most cognitive theories of counseling, for example, view resistance as intrapsychic (within the client) rather than interpersonal (Ellis 1985). Cognitive therapists view resistance as a result of the client's irrational beliefs that he is reluctant to surrender. Intrapsychic models of therapy view the problem as the client in conflict with himself and his own belief systems.

Behaviorists view resistance as a failure of the therapist to understand the client's reinforcement history rather than as an intrapsychic, internal phenomenon. The assumption is that if the therapist can apply the right set of reinforcers, the client's behavior will change. However, Wachtel (1984) noted that behaviorists increasingly recognize the role of the client's active participation in therapy, and the term "cognitive-behavioral" reflects the merging of these two theories. Behavioral concepts about the strength of immediate reinforcement and the weakness of delayed consequences to shape behavior make intuitive sense. They explain why some habits (drug addictions, for instance) are resistant to change. The immediate effect of a drug is pleasurable, and its negative effect is long delayed.

Resistance may also be viewed from the perspective of a family. Family systems theorists (Anderson and Stewart 1983) make two assumptions about families and resistance:

- First, people are influenced by the history of their family of origin and by the history of their own marital relationship.

- Second, families organize themselves both to reinforce the individual identities of their members and to ensure the survival of the family as a unit.

There is no clear consensus on the definition of resistance in family or interpersonal therapies. Similarly, there is no consensus in the intrapsychic therapies that focuses on a person's internal processing. Nevertheless, Anderson and Stewart found two common threads to organize thinking about resistance in family therapy: habit and homeostasis. A historical view of families shows ingrained, habitual, and largely unconscious patterns of one person's ways of relating to others that provide families with a sense of security and predictability. Habits and beliefs that are many years old, sometimes many generations old, will resist change. For example, members of one family recently in therapy expressed bitterness about the loss of the family plantation in the Civil War. Yet, not all beliefs and attitudes that are carried over from generation to generation are dysfunctional. Many families carry traditions of valuing education and high standards of achievement. Much of a family's and a person's ideology survives from past generations. The family is a vehicle of culture, which carries beliefs, attitudes, and values from generation to generation.

Homeostasis, on the other hand, describes a process of self-regulation by which the family maintains stability by giving corrective feedback to family members. For example, parents sometimes resist letting their children change and grow up by giving them messages to stay as they are.

Viewed at a particular moment in time, the structure of a family tends to organize itself in a particular pattern and attempts to stay that way. The family creates rules for interactions of its members, and those rules are resistant to change. For example, when children become old enough to leave home, many families create roadblocks to successful departure to keep the family as it has been. These families become stuck and unable to see new structures for their lives. Children who have been victims of incest, for example, have been indoctrinated to keep family matters secret. Long after the child has left home, these rules continue to operate. As clients, incest and other abuse victims appear resistant to counseling because the disclosure of family secrets is contradictory to ingrained family rules.

Psychodynamic theorists generally view resistance as an unconscious process of the client's defense mechanisms (denial, intellectual-ization, reaction formation, and others) that prevent awareness of unacceptable thoughts and impulses, which would be painful to explore consciously (Menninger 1958). The client's relationship with the counselor reflects these internal processes as clients transfer their issues into the therapy encounter (Strean 1985). In psychodynamic models, the resistance is viewed as intrapsychic, in contrast to the interpersonal nature of resistance in family therapy theories. However, in psychodynamic models, the resistance is viewed as primarily unconscious, while cognitive theories de-emphasize the unconscious aspects of the internal conflict and resistance to alteration of beliefs.

Indeed, an important practical issue in counseling treatment-resistant clients is whether their resistance is willful or whether it is unconscious. If a client is deliberately breaking rules of probation or terms of counseling, most counselors will tend to respond to this more harshly and judgmentally than if the client were unaware of the behavior.

Clearly, the theory of counseling and human behavior has an effect on the way they clients are perceived and counseled. Yet, for the moment, let us simply describe resistance as conflict between people, goals, or emotions (Heitler 1990). This conflict requires some expenditure of energy. It is not necessary to assume that one side in the conflict is more correct than the other. Therefore, we do not need to see the client as wrong for being in conflict with others or himself. Blanchard (1995) provided a list of such conflicts pertaining to the difficult client. He noted that a client's resistance may arise from fear or from feeling misunderstood. Resistance may stem from the therapist's poor timing, inflexibility, judgmentalness, or tendency to label the client as pathological. Resistance may be a response to coercion and threats or mistrust of the therapist's motives. The client may resist the fees being charged and may resist when he does not feel reinforced for his efforts.

Blanchard's insights are informative and practical, but it may be helpful to further categorize resistance into types. For discussion purposes, let us divide the resistances of the reluctant client into three categories:

- resistance to counseling
- resistance to change
- resistance to the counselor

This categorization may help counselors to conceptualize the treatment process. Most therapists are familiar with the concept of resistance to change and resistance to the counselor, which is often called transference. First is the central issue of resistance to counseling, that must be addressed before any constructive counseling can begin and before any needed change can occur.

Resistance to counseling is the primary resistance of the involuntary client. The client is in conflict with directives to attend counseling because he does not want to go, does not see an advantage in going, or is afraid of going. The reluctant client:

- withholds information
- misses appointments
- discredits and dismisses the counseling process
- fails to do homework assignments
- declines to cooperate with the therapist overtly or covertly

The client may be very consciously aware of his attitudes toward counseling but also may not have the ability to articulate those attitudes. Many therapists become impatient with such "resistant" behavior. They dismiss the client as unmotivated for counseling or respond irritably and try to coerce the client into appropriate behavior therapy, which sets the stage for a power struggle in therapy.

For a number of very obvious, and some not so obvious, reasons, clients resist counseling. On the top of the list is the problem of coercion. Most therapists intuitively recognize that when people are forced to do something, they usually resist. Brehm (1966) called this phenomena "psychological reactance." He noted that people display a variety of types of resistance, from passive aggressiveness to passive resistance to overt refusal, when they perceive their freedoms are being diminished. People who are forced into treatment will resent treatment per se and will resist the treatment process in some way, whether directly and openly or indirectly and covertly.

With clients who are highly reactant to coercion, it is particularly important to avoid displays of force and threats that invite power struggles between the counselor and client, creating iatrogenic (doctor-induced) resistance. In these cases, the client ends up fighting back just to retain a sense of independence and to avoid feeling subjugated by others. Confrontation with the client often fails because it gives the client the sense of losing control over himself and his choices.

Even when the counselor is acting in the client's best interest, coercion elicits negative reactions. Many of the clients who are forced into treatment have gotten into trouble precisely because they have issues with authority and with coercion. The counselor who fails to recognize this tends to activate those very same dynamics in therapy, which result in therapeutic impasses and treatment failure.

## Clients May be Reactive or Nonreactive

Obviously, it is important to be able to differentiate reactive from nonreactive clients. This is usually done on the strength of information from the client's history. Clients with long histories of conflicts with authority and/or parents are quite likely reactive. There also are clients whose overt behavior is uncooperative. They reject therapy but want and need for the counselor to provide authority and set a structure for them to follow. These nonreactive clients, however, are not typically in the position of being forced into treatment by external legal or societal pressures because they do not tend to get into the type of trouble that reactive/rebellious clients do. Nonreactive clients may be testing the therapist to see if the therapist will be strong enough and care enough to confront.

Psychological testing also may provide information about the client's attitudes and behaviors toward authority, but unless testing is done before the first session, it will not arrive in time to help the therapist early in treatment. Also, it may not be practical to use testing at the outset of every treatment case. Consequently, therapists must make their own clinical judgment about the client's reactiveness and general personality.

Another reason clients resist counseling is their basic absence of faith or trust in the power of words to resolve problems. Many clients have never had the experience of talking through problems successfully with anyone. Consequently, they harbor a deep suspicion and cynicism about talking. Clients often endorse the saying, "Talk is cheap," which implies that words do not count for much. The client views counseling as valueless because he does not believe that talk can resolve problems or lead to improvements by agreement. The counselor should be aware that this might not be the culturally accepted way to solve problems.

Of course, the central question for therapists is how to change the clients' doubts about the value of counseling. It is not likely to be helpful to merely reassure a client verbally that counseling will be different from his prior experiences. If anything, such reassurances may make him more skeptical.

Weiss (1993) suggested that perhaps clients unconsciously wish to have their false beliefs proven incorrect and want to experience with the counselor the process of working through problems by talking. To experience this, the counselor needs to build a therapeutic relationship with the client who is testing the therapist's intent by being difficult.

Processing this testing ultimately may require interpreting the transference issues, which will be discussed later, but, at least initially, the therapist may begin building a therapeutic relationship with most clients just by empathically acknowledging their doubts about the value of counseling. Sometimes, very simple reflective statements can get the discussion started. For example, a counselor might say, "You seem to be angry that you have to come here. You sound doubtful that this will help."

Many clients, of course, not only have not had successfully negotiated relationships, but they have had relationships marked by what appears to them to be deceit and lies. Children whose parents verbally profess love but who act with disregard and neglect develop a distrust of and cynicism about the spoken word. Why would such clients believe counseling would be more beneficial than talking with their parents? Again, helping clients come to accept counseling may ultimately involve dealing with the client's projections onto the therapist. For the present, note that the very idea of using language to solve problems seems questionable to many people because of their histories.

Sometimes it is helpful to explore with clients whether they have ever had a relationship in which talking helped them resolve or work through problems. This relationship may have been with a minister, a teacher, or a friend. If such a relationship has existed, exploring it may show the therapist ways to repeat the process and may remind the client of the potential of talk to be helpful. This exploration builds trust and may need to happen before the client's problems can be addressed cooperatively.

A disproportionate percentage of involuntary clients have diagnoses such as antisocial personality disorder, drug or alcohol abuse or dependence, attention deficit disorder, and other DSM-IV axis 2 personality disorders. (Even when clients have psychotic disorders, an underlying axis 2 disorder may emerge when the psychotic disorder is medicated [Meloy et al. 1990].) For example, a client whose primary diagnosis is schizophrenia may show antisocial characteristics after psychotic symptoms are treated.

A complex mix of physical and psychological factors are at play in a client's history. For example, a client who as a child was hyperactive very likely annoyed teachers and parents who attempted to control the child's behavior through threats and punishments when calm reasoning did not work. This child's experience of authority is far different from that of a child who is calm and pliable. (The child who can stay in his chair gets praise; the child who cannot gets paddled.)

Likewise, alcoholics and drug users have physical addictions that affect their mental processes. The therapist may be talking more to a chemical than a person until the client has gone through detoxification. Even then, the client's patterns of relating may have been built around the addiction to such an extent that denial may have become a way of life. Thus, some people by nature, disposition, and history are less amenable to talking through problems than others.

Another reason clients resist counseling is that they believe they should never have to do things they do not want to do. This belief is obviously related to the psychological reactance discussed earlier. It may be that some people, such as attention deficit hyperactive children, are especially oppositional or reactant to perceived pressure; it may be that oppositional characteristics are formed when people develop defenses against feeling overwhelmed and are subjugated by others who are stronger. For example, a youngster learns that saying "no" loudly deters older siblings from controlling him.

Behavioral excesses and overcompensation frequently reveal underlying fears. The homophobic male, for example, may be trying to deny feelings of warmth and attraction to other men. He may act with bravado and machismo to cover up fears of being inadequate or weak. The psychoanalytic defense mechanism of reaction formation is a similar concept. For example, a man may hide intense anger at an acquaintance by showing saccharine sweetness.

Responding to the child who behaves oppositionally and ignores rules is difficult because we want children (who are, in fact, highly dependent on adults) to develop independent thinking. We do not want to quash their attempts to be self-directive. We do not want adolescents to feel overwhelmed and threatened by adults and consequently to push away adult guidance in order to maintain and develop their own sense of self and identity. Adolescents attempt to deny their dependency by acting out. So, the therapist is constantly affirming the rebellious adolescent's push toward independence while recognizing that the child is still quite dependent. The therapist must provide support and careful structure. The therapist's task is to try to avoid provoking the client's psychological defenses that create rigid oppositional behavior.

The therapist is well advised to avoid setting a structure that cannot be enforced and creating battles that cannot be won, such as prohibiting a teenager from smoking when away from home. Generally, it is wise to avoid unnecessary rules and ultimatums, such as rules about hair length or hair styles. At the same time, therapists, often in tandem with parents, have to provide clear consequences for the violation of rules. For example, teenagers who have alcohol in their car should understand that adults have and will use their power to control access to the vehicle.

As mentioned earlier, some people believe that they should never have to do what they do not want to do. Most people recognize that such a belief is not very functional because there are so many situations in which following the guidance of others is helpful, but some people become locked into their beliefs and are unable to accept feedback from others.

A cognitive therapist might directly identify the reactive client's operative belief (that he should not have to do things) and challenge the belief with argument, but most likely this tactic will meet with resistance. The belief might be approached indirectly with Socratic or collaborative questions designed to provoke thoughtfulness:

- How did you decide that you should never have to do anthing you didn't want to do?
- Is it always true that you should never have to do what you don't want to do?
- What are the exceptions to this belief?

The problem for counseling lies in how to help clients learn when to stand up for themselves and when to follow directions. This is a tricky problem because some people are too reactant; others are too passive. The obedient child gets along well with teachers but in trying to please others loses a sense of self. In our culture, women may receive more reinforcement and encouragement for sacrificing themselves for others. Consequently, they tend to develop a different set of emotional problems than men. These include problems of neglecting self for the good of others and being too compliant with the demands of others. These clients may develop deep resentments and feel taken advantage of; nevertheless, they may see the solution to their dilemma as a change of behavior in other people. They may not see that they have the capacity to define their relationship, set limits, and refuse to continue in their caretaking role. This set of emotional problems has definite consequences for the men in their lives who are our clients.

Though we usually think of the oppositional person in discussions of treatment resistance, the overcompliant person can be just as resistant. The counselor of the reactant client is in a bind because directing the reactant client to comply with the wishes of others generates active resistance. On the other hand, a counselor directing the passive client to be more active creates contradiction. (If the therapist orders clients to act, are they acting on their own volition?) If the purpose of therapy is to help clients take responsibility for themselves, then the purpose is subverted when the counselor takes command. It is difficult but necessary to decline to give such clients too much specific direction and to allow them to struggle to take charge of their own lives.

Specifically in regard to resisting counseling, the counselor may ask clients how they decided that they should not have to be in therapy. As long as clients resent being in therapy, the likelihood of their sabotaging the process is high.

Another approach to the client's belief system would be to explore it through examining the therapy relationship, that is, through exploration of the transference issue. It is preferable to categorize this approach as resistance to the counselor rather than to counseling, but the categories overlap. The counselor, however, can explore the client's resistance to counseling by asking questions about the client's interpersonal reactions:

- What negative feelings do you have about people who make you do things?
- Do you feel angry at me because you think I am forcing you to be here?

These questions may not get honest answers. However, they provide an entry into the here-and-now concerns that the client may be able to access more easily than concerns that the counselor may identify as important therapeutic material.

Some clients quickly will be able to differentiate the counselor from a probation officer, parent, or judge and will be able to use the distinction to avoid resisting the counseling process with misdirected anger. Other clients will not be able to avoid blaming the counselor for being in counseling and will project their anger onto the therapist. These clients are probably less amenable, on the whole, to direct and rational discussion of issues. They will probably require a more process-oriented psychotherapy that uses the therapeutic relationship and the transference between client and counselor as a tool to reveal and treat the client's issues. When the client's problems are displayed in the interaction between therapist and client, they are more tangible and addressable than when they are discussed in the abstractness of the past.

The approach to the counseling process could be more beneficial if the client feels more comfortable at the beginning of a session. Sometimes, some small talk adds to the client's comfort level, and in certain cultures, such small talk is the only acceptable way for strangers to begin a dialog. Though such small talk may seem to detract precious time from the business of counseling, without it, many people would feel offended. This may be especially true with those from a Hispanic or a Native American background.

## Questions

The counselor may use the following questions to begin to address resistance to counseling:

1. What were your thoughts about coming here? (This is a cognitive-therapy type of question because it focuses on thinking and begins to train the client to be aware of and report his thoughts.).

2. When you were growing up, did you ever have the experience of solving a problem by talking with someone about it? (This question begins to explore past relationships and may prompt examination of the counselor-client relationship as well, a process that may be comfortable for psychodynamically oriented therapists.)

3. What is likely to happen if you decide not to come to counseling? (This is a practical question designed to explore consequences of behavior in a rational way.)

4. If you were not angry about being forced into therapy, what problems do you think you might identify that you would want to solve? (Sometimes, these hypothetical questions can help clients move into counseling, not by resolving their anger at being in counseling but by asking them to put the anger on hold.)

5. Do you think that you are more resentful or less resentful than other people when forced to do something? (This is a comparative question designed to elicit thoughtfulness. If successful, such questions tend to bring clients into more reflective, less reactive states.)

Rooney (1992) outlined a number of suggestions for dealing with highly reactive clients. These include the following ideas, which we will explore in detail.

- Do not label the client as a problem.
- Assist the client in restoring freedoms by clarifying choices.
- Emphasize freedoms that are retained.
- Make necessary restrictions as narrow as possible.

First, do not label the client as a problem. Rather, attribute the problem to the situation. In other words, avoid blaming the client. Though clients ultimately need to accept responsibility for themselves, they do not want to be blamed. It may sometimes be helpful to externalize the problem by giving it a name as though it were a living being. For example, the counselor may write the word "pressure" on a board and ask the client how he deals with pressure when pressure erupts. This technique often seems to separate the problem from the people involved and diffuses some of the interpersonal conflict.

Second, the counselor can assist the client in restoring threatened freedoms by clarifying choices. For example, in most situations, clients do have the option of declining counseling, though the consequences may be unacceptable. Certainly, the counselor should diligently try to help clients feel that they have some choices about how counseling will be conducted and when sessions will be scheduled.

Third, emphasize those freedoms that the client retains, such as the freedom to choose one's employment and housing. The counselor may also emphasize how lost freedoms can be restored. For example, a client who is restrained from seeing his wife may be persuaded that counseling might help the couple find ways to renew communication.

Fourth, make necessary restrictions as narrow as possible to limit reactance. For example, a probationer might be instructed to stay away from other felons rather than told to find an entirely new group of friends. Finally, people want what they cannot have. Thus, it is important not to make categorical restrictions, if at all possible.

## Practical Reasons Why Clients Don't Want Counseling

For a number of fairly practical reasons, many clients do not want to participate in counseling. These are "common sense" observations, but as Will Rogers said, what is common sense isn't often common practice.

First, counseling costs both time and money. Thus, if clients have to pay for therapy, they would probably rather not go and keep the money for other purposes. Therapists should not apologize for therapy costing money. Things that cost money have value. Clients often say "talk is cheap" as a way of dismissing the true value of counseling in contrast to its price. However, statements such as this may offer the counselor fertile grounds for exploring a client's thoughts and feelings about the worth of counseling. Therapy also costs the clients money if they must miss work to attend. It is difficult to limit the time off work to the therapy hour because it takes the client time to get to and from the appointment. Thus, a therapy hour may require several hours of commitment from the client plus time for his homework assignments.

A second practical reason that clients resist counseling is that being in counseling is a stigma for some people, especially men, who have been culturally conditioned not to appear dependent or weak (Brownell 1981). They see counseling as a process of asking others for advice, and they perceive this as a sign of weakness. It is important for the counselor to emphasize to men that they will always make the final decision for themselves and that the purpose of counseling is to explore options rather than issue directives. Many men may see counseling as a threat to their autonomy, and they are reluctant to discuss their personal issues with a stranger. Some men sexualize the therapy encounter when the therapist is a woman as a way to avoid dealing with the real issues.

Third, some clients fear that disclosures in counseling could be damaging to them. Clients may not know or understand to what extent their conversations with a therapist are confidential. It is the counselor's ethical responsibility to inform the client about the limits of confidentiality. The counselor should understand that many clients very accurately and realistically know that divulging information could hurt them if it were passed on, and they have little reason to place trust in someone they do not know.

Fourth, clients may not understand counseling well enough to know what to do. It is important to educate clients about how to be in counseling and to explain to them why it may be helpful. Exploring mutual expectations in the counseling relationship is always good.

Fifth, clients who externalize responsibility usually think someone else should be in counseling. (Though the externalizing technique discussed earlier seems to encourage the client not to own the problem, it has the curious effect of creating an entity [a nonhuman reification] with which to grapple. When clients see "the problem" as belonging to another person, such as a spouse or parent, they do not tend to participate actively in examining what they could do to change their situation.) Some clients may say that others have contributed to their problem, and thus their resistance to going through counseling alone makes some sense. The counselor's task is to not deny the contributions of other people, while focusing on the responsibilities of the client who is present for the current predicament. Likewise, clients who deny their problems without externalizing blame are not likely to see counseling as beneficial. Such clients minimize the trouble they are in and insist that they can handle it. Substance abusers are notorious for acknowledging that they use while maintaining that they suffer no negative effects from it.

Sixth, much counseling suffers from iatrogenic (doctor-induced) resistance. This occurs for a variety of reasons: therapists who are too burned out to care about the client, therapists who are angry with the client for what he may have done, or agency intake procedures that dehumanize or demean clients before they ever see the therapist. Cornelius (1994) emphasizes the importance of counselors managing stress, maintaining personal health and learning to manage their time effectively to avoid such fatigue and burnout.

## Cognitive Schemas and Resistance to Counseling

Cognitive therapists use the concept of cognitive schemas to describe fundamental core belief systems that guide the client's life (Young 1990). Examining these schemas helps counselors further understand the client who resists counseling. Schemas are similar to the transactional analysis concept of life scripts (Berne 1964). Cognitive schemas are enduring patterns of thought that guide behavior. They are resistant to change because they are ingrained and automatic in functioning. However, it may be preferable to think of schemas as merely unarticulated beliefs.

There is no commonly agreed on set of schemas, but for illustrative purposes, we will explore four domains:

- autonomy
- connectedness
- worthiness
- realistic limits

Each of these broad themes has subthemes. For example, a person with difficulties in the area of autonomy might struggle with subthemes (schemas) of dependency, subjugation, vulnerability to harm, or fear of losing self-control (Young 1990).

## Autonomy

We briefly discussed the first domain, autonomy, earlier. Clients struggling with autonomy issues may feel vulnerable to being subjugated; consequently, they develop an overreaction to defend themselves against their fears of being overwhelmed. Such clients also may be fearful of dependency. Not only are they fearful of being overpowered, but inwardly they believe they may be dependent on others, and if others are unreliable, then dependency is dangerous. To defend against this vulnerability, clients deny any dependency and fight any situation that appears to make them dependent. Thus, clients struggling with dependency issues may resist counseling because participating in it produces a feeling of being nonself-sufficient. Many men, especially, deny their need for help because they view seeking help as dependent and feminine. Clients also may reject medication or other forms of help, which they view as a crutch and a dependency.

Self-control is another variation on the autonomy theme. Many clients fear losing self-control, a theme related to subjugation. Such clients fear becoming so angry about perceived control that they react violently and without restraint. They may perceive counseling as a method of restraint, so to avoid this violent behavior, they avoid and reject the counseling.

It is critical to help coerced clients perceive that counseling will expand rather than restrict their options. People who are highly reactant psychologically will approach counseling angrily and defensively. They may resist treatment by missing appointments or refusing to talk about anything meaningful. The therapist may incorrectly perceive the behavior as resistance to talking about the specific reason for the referral when, in fact, the resistance is a more general nature, a resistance to the process of counseling itself.

The best way to help clients perceive counseling as safe depends a great deal on the therapist's personal style and theoretical orientation. It is a given that pressuring most coerced clients to talk escalates tension and increases the polarization between the counselor and the client. Once the relationship is polarized, it is difficult to reduce the distance and create a collaborative relationship.

## Connectedness

The second major domain is connectedness. Here we deal with clients' perceptions of their sense of belonging, and affiliation with significant others and with the outside world. People who have been emotionally deprived and neglected as children often experience a lack of bonding and connection to others. They mistrust other people. People who have experienced great loss or abandonment, likewise, are leery of relationships. Additionally, people who have experienced prejudice and alienation from society may be resistant to counseling, which has as its foundation the development of a trusting interpersonal relationship. Many minority clients may well bring in such mistrust to the counseling office.

The client who has struggled with trust is likely to display cynicism toward counseling. Sometimes it is helpful just to label that feeling and bring it into the open. Many treatment programs designed to treat socially unacceptable behavior (such as spousal abuse, driving under the influence) begin treatment by confronting clients with their behavior. While this may be intended to break patterns of denial, the confrontation also activates cognitive schemas related to connectedness and trust. As previously discussed, few clients who are confronted without first developing a relationship with the counselor will be able to get past the resistance to the counseling process to deal with the problem behavior. Confrontation provokes the client's cynicism and mistrust, and the client's willingness to use language to solve problems is compromised.

It would be naive of therapists to expect that reluctant clients would approach a counseling encounter with the same enthusiasm as therapists do. It is unlikely that most therapists have experienced emotional neglect or abandonment in the same way that many clients have. Yet, therapists may operate under the illusion that their clients are similar to them in their psychological make-up. Instead, it is more realistic to expect that great patience is necessary to form a trusting relationship with clients and perhaps more realistic still to accept that a deeply trusting relationship may never develop because of the limits of the client and because of the insufficient time allotted for therapy with clients.

Therapists may choose to acknowledge the client's feelings about counseling, accept them, and try to negotiate a practical agenda that is acceptable to the client. Or, the therapist may choose to try to process the core problem that is impeding the establishment of a closer therapeutic relationship. This will be difficult work. It often requires intense examination of the here-and-now relationship between the counselor and client—the transference.

Clients who are not committed to counseling because of deep personal pain or because of great external pressure seldom attend counseling sessions long enough for the processing of the transference. So, as a practical matter, it is usually wiser to assess the level of connectedness the client can develop and make realistic objectives given the client's limitations.

## Worthiness

A third core of the cognitive domain is the theme of worthiness. Clients who feel defective and unlovable sometimes seek counseling for self-esteem issues and actively seek help (though they may still resist change). However, many clients with a deeply flawed sense of worth will resist counseling to avoid having to confront the issue. They feel so defective that they are convinced that no therapy could help them. Or, they feel such shame and embarrassment that they do not believe they are even worthy of being helped. Some clients may feel they deserve to feel badly about themselves as punishment. Therefore, they reject counseling precisely because it might work.

Of course, many people cover their sense of defectiveness by feigning superiority. These clients may resist therapy because they fear it will blow their cover and undo the defenses they have constructed that at least get them through the day. These clients are well armored and difficult to approach. They may feel so incompetent as well that they dismiss counseling not because they believe it is not useful for some people but because they believe they could never make it work for themselves. Most therapists have encountered children who will not study because they do not believe they can learn. They are afraid to try to learn because if they do not succeed, it will validate their worst fears. They believe it is better not to try so that they can retain the illusion—that they are capable.

What, then, can the counselor do to help clients with such low opinions of themselves accept counseling? A common piece of advice to counselors is to be sure that clients achieve an early success in treatment to provide encouragement. While this is certainly worth keeping in mind, it is doubtful that an early success or two will help the client overcome a deeply ingrained belief in his self-image. It may be useful to explore the resistance to counseling by directly asking clients whether they believe they could benefit from counseling.

Ironically, such a direct question often results in good material for counseling more quickly than addressing the specific reason for the referral. For example, take the case of a client referred because of an arrest for shoplifting. It would be tempting to try to explore the nature of the incident and try to encourage discussion on the problems stemming from the incident. However, the client may not understand his impulse to steal and may not feel that it can be controlled. (Certainly many addicts and alcoholics feel pessimistic that they can control their habits because they have tried to stop by themselves so many times before and have failed.) Exploring clients' pessimism about the current treatment process stemming from prior failures to change is probably a more effective way to talk clients into examining why they are resisting counseling now.

In many types of therapy, from solution-focused approaches to cognitive therapy, the therapist tries to get the client to identify an agenda for the current session. The problem, as previously discussed, is that the involuntary client does not want to do this. Consequently, a therapist who wants to be effective with such clients will have to make some guesses about roadblocks to collaborative work and then directively explore these themes.

## Realistic Limits

Being unable to set realistic limits is the last core of the cognitive domain in resistance to counseling. Clients with acting-out problems of various kinds occupy this group. They often display a sense of entitlement, few inhibitions, and insufficient control. They narcissistically object to restrictions, which they see as perhaps applying to others but not to themselves. These clients are discussed in greater length in the section on antisocial behavior.

First, such clients are generally difficult to retain and contain in outpatient counseling without sufficient external leverage, such as court orders. The therapist has to structure counseling fairly tightly to avoid being abused by noncompliance problems, such as failure to come for sessions. If there are no consequences for not coming, then a client of this type will not show up.

On the other hand, if the counselor has leverage to use, the danger exists of provoking a power struggle. Some therapists do not like to use authority and power to force clients to work in treatment (Palmer 1983), but such leverage can be approached carefully and matter-of-factly. For example, counselors can politely tell the client that they will not provide a positive report to a probation officer unless certain tasks are done.

Counselors should be at ease in defining the limits of their own behavior. It is unwise to lie for the client by saying that the client is progressing in counseling if, in fact, this is not the case. If the consequence of this to the client is that his probation is provoked, that is the way it is. After taking these stands, if the client has an external pressure to remain in counseling, then a discussion can develop about the fairness of the coercion and the rights of other people relative to the client.

Yochelson and Samenow's work on the criminal personality (1976, 1977) conceptualizes an approach to clients whose conduct appeared essentially irresponsible. These clients' thoughts and assumptions about the world are so different from therapists' that it is difficult for the therapist to understand the client's meaning. For example, this writer was frustrated during the Watergate investigation when his inmate clients were irate that Nixon had broken the law. It was hard to understand how these drug dealers, rapists, and assorted other law violators could be so indignant at Nixon but complacent about themselves until it became clear that they believed rules apply only to other people.

The recognition of the criminal's way of thinking prompted discussions with clients about their fundamental worldviews and the basis and consequences for such views. This type of counseling is philosophical and enjoyable, but few clients voluntarily choose to engage in it unless there is an external threat that is clear and present (Samenow 1984). Their reluctance to engage in this type of counseling is due to their initial resistance to all counseling. Chapter 7 contains further discussion of the criminal personality.

Other clients who appear to have little regard for boundaries and limits on their behavior may be interpreted as trying to provoke an authority figure to provide guidance and protection as their parents never did. Many clients who had neglectful parents want the comfort of a firm but caring therapist. Such clients will often drop out of therapy but will respond positively to a therapist calling to express concern and encouragement for them to return to therapy.

It is important to try to distinguish between the client who has little self-discipline and poor boundaries because of having been neglected and the client who has developed an entitled worldview through other developmental processes. Unfortunately, their behaviors are identical, and therapists will disagree about the genesis of the problems. When this happens in institutional settings, staff become divided. Some staff take a supportive role; others become punitive.

People respond to their core schemas in several ways. The first way is to find methods to maintain and confirm the schema. The person looks for and may even create evidence that the schema is true. For example, the client who struggles with autonomy issues sees all the ways that counseling is restrictive and oppressive. He may behave in ways to activate restrictive and oppressive behavior in the counselor. In this way, the client remains dependent, which confirms his long-held belief.

The second way that people deal with core schemas is to overcompensate for them. The client struggling with autonomy issues, for example, refuses to accept help and tries to remain supremely independent. This struggle reveals his underlying fear of dependency.

A third way that clients deal with core schemas is to avoid situations that activate their examination of the schema. For example, the client struggling with autonomy schemas avoids counseling by missing appointments or even refusing to come.

Responses to schemas are seldom solely behavioral, cognitive, or affective, but may be primarily one or the other. For example, the man who avoids situations that would activate the processing of schemas is responding primarily in a behavioral way; however, this behavior leads him to avoid experiencing the issue in any cognitive or affective way, as well. Similarly, when schema-maintenance behavior occurs, it also has an active cognitive and affective process.

These conceptual tools for understanding resistance to counseling lead to practical interventions. In the next chapter there is a discussion about applying the concepts discussed so far to the introductory therapy session with the treatment-resistant client.

# Chapter 3

## The First Session With a Treatment-Resistant Client

*P*revious chapters dealt with themes related to treatment resistance, including the implications of involuntariness on therapy; the twin issues of denial and externalizing blame; and basic resistance to counseling, resistance to change, and resistance to the counselor. These chapters examined several different theoretical ways of conceptualizing resistance, including the cognitive therapy constructs of cognitive schemas. This chapter provides the nuts and bolts for what to do in preliminary sessions. It is broken down into the five following steps:

1. Assess the client
2. Deal with the issue of voluntariness
3. Challenge false beliefs
4. Find a problem on which the client will agree to work
5. Develop a treatment plan

## Assess the Client

Some type of formal or informal assessment happens in every counseling encounter. Counselor and client size each other up and behave according to their perceptions. It may not be essential to conduct extensive psychological testing. Brief therapy models almost preclude allowing time for such assessment, and problem- and solution-focused models do not emphasize the importance of personality constructs on the conduct of therapy. However, at a minimum, there should be some assessment of the client's capacity to engage in counseling and his willingness to work.

Clients with formal thought disorders (such as schizophrenia) usually are not good subjects for therapy until they receive psychiatric care, usually medication. The primary recommendation of Meloy et al. (1990) is for counselors of psychiatrically disabled clients to work as part of an interdisciplinary team that includes a psychiatrist.

With this group, much of the counselor's job is to explain to the client the importance of the medication and to work through the client's resistance to taking and staying on medication. As previously noted, the client's resistance to taking medication may stem from his fears of dependency. Once thought disorders are treated, personality disorders may become more evident. It is important to be prepared for these dual-diagnosis clients.

Many other "dual diagnosis" problems exist with resistant clients, and psychiatric help may be useful. Many substance abusing clients have underlying mood disorders, such as depression, that may be medically treatable. The substance abuse may be an attempt by the client to self-medicate, and it does not make sense to treat the underlying medical problem with psychotherapy. Other conditions are not so clearly biological in origin, but they may still respond to medication. For example, some clients who have anger- or impulse-control problems may respond to mood levelers, and when treated, they often become more amenable to psychotherapy.

Whenever there is any question about whether medical intervention may be helpful, get a medical consultation. It is increasingly apparent that there are biological, psychological, and social influences on behavior, and difficult cases call for a consideration of all possibilities (Lazarus 1992).

A second important assessment consideration is the extent to which the client has a diagnosable personality disorder. Whether the therapist finds such personality disorder labels useful, these concepts are not meaningless. Clearly, some personalities with a pathological outlook are quite different from most clients. The antisocial client who disregards the rights of others is a case in point. Such clients do not establish true interpersonal bonds. It is usually a mistake to assume that empathy with them will allow the counselor to forge a therapeutic relationship.

Of course, it is important to be clear about appropriate boundaries with all clients. Clients with personality disorders often try to use the counselor's caring as a weapon. For example, the client may try to extract favors and privileges that the counselor should not grant. In a correctional institution, for example, the client may ask to use the counselor's phone. A probationer may ask the counselor to verify attendance at sessions that he did not, in fact, attend. Consequently, from the beginning, the counselor should have some idea whether the client is antisocial in order to be able to select a suitable approach. It is important to be especially clear about appropriate boundaries with these clients.

Though there is much disagreement about this issue, Yochelson and Samenow (1976) are correct in their assertion that the counselor of antisocial clients with criminal personalities must be more dispassionate than empathic. The problems of the personality-disordered client are fairly deeply ingrained. This makes it vitally important that the therapist working with the client in limited sessions clearly specifies issues to be addressed. Otherwise, therapy time becomes scattered and poorly focused as scores of issues bubble up and are minimally addressed in the allotted time.

Effective therapy with personality-disordered clients requires deeper psychotherapy than brief therapy allows. Yochelson and Samenow's (1976) approach required one year of daily three-hour group treatment. If there is not enough time allocated to do this intensive therapy, then therapy goals need to be modified to fit within the allowed schedule.

Therapy goals also should be modified to be consistent with the counselor's skill level. In-depth therapy in psychodynamic models involves confronting the client's behavior toward the counselor as a way to examine underlying personality dynamics. Examining this transference is slow and difficult work that many counselors are not prepared to do and do not have time to do.

Other clients have problems in living. These are the clients most counselors see. This broad category includes people with substance abuse problems, though these problems can be as intractable as those of either thought or personality disordered clients. Dowd and Wallbrown (1993) describe the personality of the psychologically reactant client, including dynamics of motivation and relationships, which are of interest to counselors and therapists. They administered the Therapeutic Reactance Scale, the Questionnaire for Measuring Psychological Reactance, and the Personality Research Form to 251 undergraduate students. They concluded that the psychologically reactant person tends to be aggressive, dominant, defensive, autonomous, and is quick to take offense. Such persons do not affiliate with others and do not to seek or give support. The reactant person values freedom from restraint.

Though these descriptions sound quite negative, the authors also noted that, in some circumstances, such people might be forceful and effective leaders. They may have great confidence in themselves. They would try to control events rather than be controlled. Counseling would be difficult, because they would not be easily influenced by the counselor.

In the *DSM-IV* (1994), the diagnosis of passive-aggressive personality disorder was removed. However, this diagnosis in the *DSM-IIIR* was very descriptive of a large number of reactive, treatment-resistant clients. The *DSM-IIIR* described these clients as having a pervasive pattern of passive resistance to demands for social and occupational performance. This included procrastinating, becoming sulky and argumentative when asked to do something, working slowly to avoid unpleasant tasks, protesting that demands were unreasonable, "forgetting" obligations, evaluating personal performance higher than others did, resisting suggestions from others, obstructing the efforts of others by failing to participate, and unreasonably criticizing or scorning people in positions of authority.

Given these descriptions of reactant people, it is easy to speculate what problems in living they might have. These might include brushes with authority and difficult interpersonal relationships. Clearly, a major task for the counselor is assessing how reactive a client is and planning an approach in counseling that avoids activating counter-productive behaviors. There is no point in setting unnecessary limits, because this brings about damaging defiance.

Like the antisocial client, the reactant client may have problematic interpersonal relationships. Unlike the antisocial client, the reactant client may have the capacity to form a productive therapeutic alliance. So, it may be helpful to empathize with the reactant client's feelings of anger when he feels constrained or restricted. This is less true with antisocial clients who do not develop any mutuality or sense of reciprocity in relationships.

## Deal With Issues of Involuntariness

A second task in the beginning work with a coerced or treatment-resistant client is to deal with the issue of involuntariness. As previously described, it may be helpful to empathize with the anger the client feels at being coerced into counseling. Empathy tends to further the therapeutic alliance by helping the client to feel understood. Such behavior also helps to disassociate the counselor from the source of the coercion and helps the client understand that the therapist does not mandate the therapy.

The counselor should be careful not to reject the moral or legal basis for the coercion. That is, if the requirement to be in counseling is legitimate, the counselor cannot disagree with the court or authority making the requirement. Nevertheless, it is important to understand the client's feelings. Most counselors do not enjoy wielding power over their clients, though for probation and parole officers and corrections' counselors, power is inherent in the job. However, whenever possible, counselors should disassociate from power and coercion because counseling should empower clients, not control them.

Counselors should also learn whether clients will blame them for the coercion. Counselors should assess how strongly they adhere to their beliefs and should point out that they are not the ones who ordered the counseling to take place. Most clients will recognize this and not be angry at the therapist. Clients who persist in blaming the therapist probably have core issues that will require longer-term therapy and indirect approaches.

When clients acknowledge some responsibility for their predicament, it is possible for counseling to be direct. However, when clients project their problems onto therapists irrationally, the counselor needs to remain somewhat hidden by asking questions, getting information, and encouraging the client to talk. The transference relationship between counselor and client becomes a focus of counseling and also a gauge of progress. That is, the more accurately and realistically the client treats the counselor, the more progress is occurring. Yet, if the client treats the counselor as a parent, difficult problems remain.

## Challenge False Beliefs

At some point in counseling, the therapist begins to challenge the client's false beliefs. These challenges may be direct or indirect, depending on the openness of the client to challenge. Reactive clients respond to challenges by locking into a power struggle, but less obvious confrontations may be helpful. Ellis (1985) acknowledged that when vigorous persuasion sets up resistance to the counselor, the counselor should return to relationship building. As long as the client has an external adversary, there is no internal scrutiny. While a head-on clash with the client may be counterproductive, there are other approaches to take to begin to undermine false beliefs.

The false beliefs that undermine participation in counseling fall into three major areas that demand challenging:

- low-frustration tolerance
- discomfort anxiety
- narcissistic resistance

**Low-Frustration Tolerance.** Clients with low-frustration tolerance often believe that they should not have to exert much effort to satisfy the requirements of counseling or to change. Of course, anyone can agree that it would be nice for everything to be easy, but the counselor can at least ask clients why they believe things should be easier than they are. The counselor may need to ask clients if they have such a belief. This method will enable the client to surface the issue and identify it. It is not always necessary to argue that such a belief is untrue, though this direct approach may be effective, at times. Clients who are spending their energy being distressed at how difficult things are seldom have enough energy to apply to actually solving problems, so it is important to deal with their low-frustration tolerance.

**Discomfort Anxiety**. A second belief counselors need to challenge is discomfort anxiety. Clients with discomfort anxiety often have substance abuse problems and use drugs or alcohol to relieve anxiety caused by a variety of life events. When clients tell themselves, "I can't stand to feel anxious" about a problem or conflict, they solve their problem by treating it with a chemical (Ellis 1985). Beck et al. (1993) identified a variety of addictive beliefs, such as the expectation that a substance will improve intellectual functioning; increase pleasure; have a soothing effect; relieve boredom, anxiety, tension, and depression; and satisfy cravings. They also identified permission-giving beliefs such as, "Since I'm feeling bad, it's ok to use" and "If I take a hit, I can get away with it," and "I'm entitled." All of these beliefs center around the person's inability to tolerate discomfort.

Since most effective counseling at some time increases discomfort, it is essential to deal with beliefs that impede tolerating discomfort. If the client will permit a direct examination of these thoughts and beliefs without it threatening the therapeutic relationship, then the counselor can ask direct questions and point out the fallacy in the client's thinking. However, if the client is highly reactive and the therapeutic relationship is fragile, then it is more important to challenge the beliefs more subtly by asking what evidence the client has to support the belief. Often, just asking clients to explain themselves is sufficient to provoke an examination that begins to undermine their former thinking.

**Narcissistic Resistance**. The third category of false belief that counselors must challenge early in counseling is narcissistic resistance to counseling. Clients often believe that they should be able to do what they want, when they want to do it; they should not have to do anything they do not want to do, and they should be treated "fairly." Such clients have difficulties with setting or obeying realistic limits, one of the core schemas discussed earlier. As long as clients are angry that they are being restricted, it is difficult to get them to examine other changes that they need to make.

Clients who reject limits on themselves seem particularly difficult to engage in counseling because they project blame so readily onto others. Their view is that they would be fine if others would just leave them alone. Sometimes it is helpful to look for exceptions to their rules. That is, ask if there are any circumstances in which conforming to rules is reasonable, such as obeying traffic laws. Most clients will acknowledge the need to obey traffic laws. The counselor, then, can begin to ask what other rules the client finds reasonable, what rules he finds unreasonable and why. These discussions can be philosophical, but they can eventually come full circle to examining the reasonableness of being required to participate in counseling.

## Find a Problem On Which the Client Will Agree to Work

Probably more important than anything else, it is important to define a problem or goal on which the client agrees to work. When clients voluntarily seek counseling, they come with an issue or feeling they want to change. There may be unconscious roadblocks to change, but at least the client can identify the subject of the counseling. Coerced and treatment-resistant clients see the problems as external to themselves. So, when the counselor asks what needs changing, the client points a finger at someone else who cannot be influenced in the counseling session. The counselor must find a way to frame a topic that can be addressed in counseling.

The art of counseling difficult clients is to gradually shift the responsibility back to the client. One technique for doing this is through detached questioning. In detached questioning the counselor continues to ask clients to define their role in a problem. For example, if the client denies responsibility for a fight with a friend, the counselor can ask questions to get specific, factual information about the chain of events that led to the fight, including the client's specific behaviors. This can be done without directly implying blame, but the questioning points clearly to the client's involvement.

In the early counseling sessions, the task of finding a mutually agreeable focus is a broad one. It only requires the identification of things that the client wishes were different. The most obvious problem the client has is being under pressure to be in counseling. When clients deny having problems, they usually believe they do not have problems with which they think the counselor can help. The following script demonstrates finding a problem focus:

| | |
|---|---|
| **Counselor**: | What problems do you want to focus on here in counseling? |
| Client: | I don't know. I don't think I have any problems. |
| **Counselor**: | Well, it seems to me that one of the problems you have is having to be in counseling. |
| Client: | Well, yeah, but there's nothing you can do about that. |
| **Counselor**: | Maybe. But I suspect you're angry about it. Do you like feeling angry? |
| Client: | No, but that's the way it is. |
| **Counselor**: | Do you think it would be worthwhile to see if there's a way to deal with your anger about it constructively? |
| Client: | Maybe. |
| **Counselor**: | Have you ever been angry before at being made to do something? |
| Client: | Sure, but that's how it is when people force you to do what they want. |
| **Counselor**: | What different ways have you dealt with that kind of pressure? |
| Client: | Sometimes, I ignore it. Sometimes, I get mad. |
| **Counselor**: | When you've ignored it in the past, did you get away with it? |
| Client: | Sometimes. |
| **Counselor**: | So maybe what we need to do is figure out when it's safe to ignore demands from other people and when it's not. Do you think everybody hates being forced to do things as much as you do? |
| Client: | Yeah, I guess. |
| **Counselor**: | How do you know? Is it possible they don't? |
| Client: | Maybe. |
| **Counselor**: | Maybe it would be helpful to understand why you are particularly sensitive to pressure. |
| Client: | Yeah, I do get pretty mad. |

In this scene, the client has been introduced to the notion of using counseling to look at himself and to examine differences between himself and others. Rather than preaching self-responsibility to the client, the counselor tries to frame the problem in a way that allows the client to enter into counseling without losing face. If clients feel boxed in by the questions, their answers will remain terse, so it is important to encourage clients to feel free to express their thoughts and feelings by remaining nonjudgmental.

Many therapists may be making their work with treatment-resistant clients more difficult than it needs to be by ignoring straightforward and simple interventions with these clients. For example, when a client seems to be holding back by not talking, the counselor might try simply reflecting that observation, making the covert become overt. If done nonconfrontationally, the client has the option to deny or acknowledge the observation.

Even if the client denies such behavior, the client knows that the counselor knows what is happening, and the passive-resistant behavior loses some of its power. If clients choose to acknowledge the restraint, the counselor can ask clients why they need to remain silent. Talking about not talking can be a very powerful tool to explore clients' fears about counseling and to identify problems that are the usual focus of therapy. Remember, clients will not identify problems for therapy if they are still resisting the idea of counseling itself.

When clients agree to participate, they only agree to work on issues that they see as important. Many therapists like to develop contracts with clients that spell out the terms of counseling. These contracts are a good idea but only if the client clearly perceives a quid pro quo arrangement; that is, if the contract is forced on the client without the client's input, the contract is useless.

Clients must perceive that they are getting something in exchange for their effort. An example of a flawed arrangement is the typical probation contract that unilaterally spells out the terms of probation. Clients who sign these "agreements" are not really agreeing to anything. They sign because they are forced to, not because they think the arrangement is fair. Consequently, the odds are slim that they will comply with the contract.

Ideally, contracts with clients should be physically written in the client's own handwriting and language. The greater the participation by the client, the greater are the chances for success. In practice, many situations require that the therapist complete the paperwork, but therapists should be aware that the more they do the work, the less the client has invested in the process (Goodyear and Bradley 1980).

A variation to finding a problem to work on is to find a solution. Selekman (1993) offered suggestions for working with difficult adolescents by employing a brief solution-oriented approach. As with other counseling theories, rapport building is essential, and beginning efforts are aimed at establishing a therapeutic alliance by using self-disclosure, humor, therapeutic compliments, normalizing, and positive relabeling. For example, a withdrawn adolescent can be positively relabeled as thoughtful, or an angry parent's behavior can be portrayed as showing a high level of concern and commitment.

A primary assumption of solution-oriented therapy is that clients have the ability to solve their dilemmas and that problems are unsuccessful attempts to resolve difficulties. Nevertheless, the focus on problems is inevitably negative while focusing on desired outcomes is encouraging and positive. So, instead of dwelling on defining what is wrong and how it got that way, the solution-oriented therapist asks outcome questions, such as:

- If a miracle happened in your sleep tonight and solved all your problems, how would you be able to tell tomorrow that a miracle must have happened?
- How would your life be different if all your problems were solved?
- If you were living your life the way you wanted it and you made a movie, tell me what scenes I would see.

By focusing on solutions, the therapist can help the client define in specific terms how to achieve the desired goal or outcome without necessarily spending a great deal of time on the depressing details that led to the client's current situation. Brief–session therapists believe that even small changes will become amplified and lead to larger eventual changes. A therapist who wants to work from a solution orientation can do so with the treatment-resistant client and may find that the approach pays dividends and avoids the negativity of focusing on problems and pathology.

## Develop a Treatment Plan

Most therapists find it helpful to develop an overview of the resistances a particular client seems to have. This overview can easily develop into a treatment plan. Using three sheets of paper, the counselor can identify the resistances to counseling, to change, and to the counselor. For example, the counselor lists on the first page in one column all the reasons the counselor suspects the client may be resisting counseling, such as fear of disclosure, cost, and so on. On the second page, the counselor lists the client's reasons for not wanting to change. This speculating does not need to be theory based but should be as specific as possible. For example, the counselor may write that the client does not want to change because he believes he does not have any problems or because he does not think changing would help his situation. On the third page, the counselor records the reasons the client may resist the counselor. For example, the counselor represents authority or coercion.

Having identified the client's resistances to counseling, change, and the counselor in a treatment plan, the counselor may try to empathize with these resistances, especially the resistances to change, by listing the disadvantages of not resisting. (Many counselors have difficulty with this exercise because it is counter-intuitive, but it is very helpful.) For example, for a person with an alcohol problem, the counselor should list some possible disadvantages of resisting or participating in the change process. (See Appendix A, B, and C for exercises on reasons for resisting and identifying ambivalence about change.) First, the client would have to get new friends because all his old friends are drinking partners. Not only is this hard work but it is anxiety producing. Finding nondrinking friends requires new places to socialize and a whole new set of social activities. People who have never socialized without the benefit of alcohol often do not know how to stand, talk, mingle, and act when sober. A married client who has used alcohol to numb anger at a spouse might have to learn to deal with that anger or be at risk of expressing the anger in a dangerous way. The client might consider it safer to continue to drink than to be sober. At a minimum, the client would have to make some decisions about whether to remain in the relationship, and for most people, the thought of leaving a relationship, even a bad one, is distressing.

At a deeper level, a disadvantage of changing is that the client would have to develop a new self-concept of himself as a person who does not drink. This is no small matter for someone who has oriented his life around the next drink and who has dealt with most emotions by numbing them with alcohol. Psychodynamic therapists conceptualize resistances as the stubborn persistence of the personality to satisfy basic drives. Or, in newer psychodynamic theories (Weiss 1993), psychotherapists postulate that resistance stems from the obstacles to changing one's basic dysfunctional beliefs about the world, even if the individual wishes to do so. Regardless of the theoretical frame of reference, it is possible for the counselor to see the inherent difficulty the client will face with change and empathize with the client's concerns.

Therapy with people with "bad habits" (smoking, for instance), unfortunately, often degenerates into the therapist imploring the client to stop. This, of course, does not work. Clients struggle against the counselor as they have against probably dozens of others who have attempted to change them. It is more effective to empathize with clients by identifying the reasons why they will have difficulty changing. This empathy helps the client feel understood, and, paradoxically, permits the client to embrace the possibility of change. If the counselor tells the client to change, the client answers by saying why it is not possible. If the counselor empathizes with the difficulties in the path of change, the client can focus on the need for change.

Paradoxical directives are sometimes effective for behaviorally defiant clients (Tennen et al. 1981; Frankl 1960). For example, a client who is suspicious of a therapist might be encouraged to be especially careful and supported in his notion that it is important to be careful about trusting people until they are better known. However, paradoxical behavioral directives have the potential to backfire, and they may rely too much on gimmicks for some therapists. For example, it is obviously dangerous to challenge a suicidal client to go ahead and jump. Empathy, on the other hand, is a commonly recognized core condition of effective therapy, and supreme empathy (taking empathy to its logical conclusion) is quite paradoxical by itself. When a counselor empathizes with the many reasons the client identifies for not being able to make a change, the client often begins to argue why change is necessary, after all, as the following example shows:

| Counselor: | I can see how difficult it would be for you to not be angry at your wife. If you didn't get mad, you're concerned that she would control everything in your relationship. |
| --- | --- |
| Client: | Yeah, she does try to run my life. I'm not gonna put up with that. |
| Counselor: | You feel you've got a right to be angry and threatening. You'd rather have her call the cops on you than have her call the shots. |
| Client: | Yeah, but I don't want the cops in the middle of my life either. |
| Counselor: | But you'd rather have the police come than feel controlled by your wife, and you can't find a way to work things out with your wife without getting angry. |
| Client: | Yeah, but I need to do something. |
| Counselor: | But how can you work things out and still feel like a man? You don't see any way to do that. |
| Client: | Yeah, that's right. But if I don't do something, she'll leave me for good or I'll be in jail. |

It seldom works out so easily with reluctant clients identifying what they need to do. Unfortunately, it is quite predictable that clients will defeat the therapist's attempts to identify the "right" course of action. The following chapters review research on therapy with treatment-resistant clients to establish some general principles.

# Chapter 4

# Research on Psychotherapy Effectiveness and Involuntary Treatment

*D*espite the many theories of psychotherapy, a great deal of evidence points to key ingredients in successful counseling. Many authors, of course, emphasize the importance of the therapeutic relationship. Lambert (1992) summarized psychotherapy outcome research, saying that approximately 30 percent of change was attributable to common factors in therapy such as empathy, warmth, acceptance, and encouragement of risk taking. Specific techniques of therapy were credited with only 15 percent of change. Extratherapeutic factors (client social support, environmental factors, and others) accounted for 40 percent of change. What the client believed would happen accounted for the remaining 15 percent.

## The Role of Empathy in Therapeutic Outcome

Support, learning, and action factors are associated with positive outcomes and are common across therapies (Lambert 1992). The support factor includes: development of catharsis; identification with the therapist; reassurance; mitigation of isolation; release of tension; and therapist warmth, respect and trust. Lambert's review of the literature concluded that at least 30 percent of change in therapy was attributable to the common factors, including the support factor. Thus, it is apparent that therapists who want to be effective with treatment-resistant clients will need to find ways to create a level of empathy and support.

The relationship of the patient and therapist is crucial to outcome (Garfield 1992). Seventy percent of clients rated five items as very important to them in therapy:

- the therapist's personality
- the therapist helping the client to understand the problem
- the therapist encouraging the client to gradually practice facing things
- being able to talk to an understanding person
- the therapist helping the client to understand self

Once again, studies of therapeutic effectiveness show the therapeutic relationship is crucial regardless of the particular theoretical orientation of the therapist. This makes the development of empathy more crucial for counselors of treatment-resistant clients. For example, Young (1992), in his presentation of eclectic psychotherapy, placed the therapeutic relationship as the axle around which the other spokes of the therapeutic wheel revolved. He noted that all therapy consisted of helping clients with self-esteem, gaining new experiences, learning, activating expectations and motivation, lowering or raising emotional arousal, and practicing new behavior. The presence of a therapeutic relationship was necessary for any technique in these other areas.

The counseling of mandated clients inevitably poses problems in developing a mutually understanding relationship because of one crucial difference between the counselor and the client: one chooses to be present and the other does not. In *A Day in the Life of Ivan Denisovich*, the author, Alexander Solzhenitsyn (1963), posed the question of whether a guard could understand an inmate in the Soviet concentration camp—because how could a man who is warm understand a man who is cold? Similarly, it is crucial that the counselor above all else try to understand the loss of human dignity that accompanies any type of coercion.

Ironically, clients who are enraged by coercion may be showing the essence of the human spirit: the desire to be free and self-determining. Counselors can value this spirit in their clients, while recognizing that there are inevitable limits to freedom and responsibilities that accompany freedom. There is a difference between the desire to be free and the desire to be free of consequences. The benefits of freedom should not come at others' expense.

The difficulties of developing empathy with difficult clients occur for a variety of specific reasons. The therapist may find it hard to relate to clients who come from poor socioeconomic classes or who are from different races than the counselor. This is a special problem when the bulk of therapists are white, and they counsel treatment-resistant clients, many of whom are minorities. Soriano (1995) contended that the race of the counselor does not have a significant effect on therapy outcome, as long as the therapist is culturally sensitive, but other writers (Chin 1993) are less sanguine in their appraisal of the interchangeableness of therapists. Substantial evidence shows that race may affect whether clients are referred to therapeutic programs or programs that are more punitive in nature (Johansen 1983; Harris and Kirk 1983; Diuguid 1995). Thus, it is important for therapists to take cultural, demographic and socioeconomic factors into consideration at all stages of treatment. The American Psychological Association's position paper (1990) provides a balanced appraisal of the literature on this subject.

Two major variables differentiating client and counselor include demographics and interpersonal response patterns (Beutler and Consoli 1992). Their review of research concluded that an initial slight (but not large) dissimilarity of beliefs and values between counselor and client is beneficial for change. Demographic similarities tend to improve positive perceptions, retention in therapy, and treatment adherence, but, ironically, these similarities did not seem to contribute to therapy outcome. However, widely disparate beliefs and values between counselor and client were negative predictors of outcome.

Little research or evidence suggests when a male or female counselor would be preferable. However, Erickson (1993) has written a thorough examination to help prepare women for working with men. Men sometimes attempt to sexualize the relationship with female therapists, and women need to be well prepared to set appropriate boundaries. Women clients may also try to sexualize the counseling relationship by being seductive or dependent. Male counselors must also be prepared to set appropriate limits in therapy.

The reality in clinical practice is that there often will be major differences in demographic as well as interpersonal factors between the counselor and the client. In prison settings, for example, it is unlikely that the therapists will come from the socioeconomic class of most inmates. Clients from impoverished backgrounds may have little understanding of the concept of saving money or investing for the future. Clients from working class families may have had exposure only to employment in which there was an hourly wage. These clients might be uncomfortable with vocational counseling exploring anything but hourly employment. This is a difficult issue because most counselors are probably not able to advise clients on being self-employed or entrepreneurial. Many counselors have never worked in sales or commission-based positions. Nevertheless, counseling may perpetuate the client's limited view of vocational possibilities if a range of ways of making a living is not discussed. Counselors may better prepare themselves by reading about small business ownership and entrepreneurial businesses.

Sometimes, counselors from modest backgrounds find themselves working with clients who come from great wealth. Drug and alcohol counselors, for example, may have clients whose wealth has permitted and sustained not only the substance abuse but a narcissism and sense of entitlement and privilege that interferes with their treatment. Correctional counselors working with white-collar offenders also may have clients who come from powerful positions and wealth. These clients may view the counselor with disdain, and the counselor may feel intimidated by the client's previous status and position (Harris 1987).

Counselors need to recognize their own values, prejudices, and biases and attempt to identify their blind spots. Counselors also should be prepared to admit that there are some clients who they do not like (Duehn and Proctor 1977; Pekarik and Blodgett 1986; Rupple and Kaul 1982; Paradise and Wilder 1979; Vontress 1974). Will Rogers said he never met a man he didn't like, but most of us are less tolerant. It is better to have an honest recognition of one's feelings than to be phony and not genuine. It may not be possible or wise for counselors to try to hide their feelings entirely, but it is not necessary to directly express such feelings either in the beginning of counseling. Often, if the counselor can gather information professionally, a working relationship can be formed, and the counselor can develop empathy for the client. However, if counselors are aware of their continuing negative reactions to the client, there may be a need for supervision and assistance with their feelings and, eventually, for referral of the client to another counselor. Some of the counselor's counter-transference reactions to difficult clients may be difficult to overcome.

Unfortunately, the client who is abrasive or rebellious creates a variety of counter-transference reactions in the therapist that often block communication of empathy. Meloy (1990) listed several therapist counter-transference reactions. The first is therapeutic nihilism. The therapist becomes hopeless and pessimistic that any therapy can help. A second therapist reaction is excessive fear of personal harm. This causes the therapist to be paralyzed and ineffective. A third reaction is vicarious satisfaction over client rebellion, which often leads to a tacit encouragement of inappropriate behavior. A fourth therapist reaction is one of rage about the devaluation and hatred expressed by the client.

Therapists also may try too hard to develop empathy by creating an illusion of the existence of a therapeutic alliance when none exists and by assuming that the client shares common values (Meloy et al. 1990). Some of the difficulty in forging a therapeutic alliance lies in the inability of the counselor to empathize with the client and to understand the client's differences.

Research has indicated that self-referred clients were half as likely to terminate counseling as other-referred clients (Pekarik 1986). Counselors' counter-transference reactions contribute to premature termination from therapy. Most patients terminate therapy before all problems have been addressed and resolved (Lazarus 1992). Though this is the rule rather than the exception, it does not mean that the therapist should contribute to the early departure by irritating clients with unproductive countertransference. Some therapists contend that it may be preferable to terminate counseling abruptly rather than allow it to peter out because such an approach may encourage the client to consider returning at a later date (Young 1992). Premature termination is an often overlooked area for research in psychotherapy (Ward 1984). It is important for the counselor to explore with prematurely terminating clients their reasons and feelings for wanting to stop (Young 1992).

Beutler and Consoli (1992) provided further clarification of research on what works with difficult clients. They identified basic dimensions to be considered: problem severity and complexity, reactance level, and coping style. They then suggested guidelines for therapy with various types of clients.

First, the authors argued that complex problems require a broad-based treatment plan aimed at conflict resolution. When clients have ongoing patterns of dysfunctioning, it is important to address the underlying themes in conflict. However, when the problem is situation specific and the client has generally had a history of being able to manage anxiety and conflict, specific problem/symptom resolution is required. These recommendations have obvious implications that dictate when brief therapy is indicated and contra-indicated, since brief approaches are most appropriate for clients without long histories of conflict. Many involuntary clients do, in fact, have long histories of conflict, so it may be argued that brief therapy is often inappropriate for them. On the other hand, if time is limited and surface problems can be identified to discuss, then brief therapy may be adequate. However, there should be no pretense of effecting deep personality change.

Beutler and Consoli continued their analysis by identifying four basic coping styles: internalizing, externalizing, repressive, and cyclic. An internalizing coping style is characterized by self-blame and self-devaluation. An externalizer attributes blame to others. Repressive individuals invest their resources in maintaining a general lack of awareness. Cyclic styles are displayed by clients who are behaviorally unstable. They fluctuate from internalization to externalization. These coping styles interact with their reactance level.

Beutler and Consoli made the following recommendations for therapy:

- With repressive clients, insight-oriented therapies are most effective.
- With internalizing clients, procedures that improve emotional arousal and awareness are most effective.

- With cyclic clients whose moods are labile and whose behavior is volatile, procedures that improve cognitive self-control are most effective.
- With externalizing clients, use procedures that maximize behavioral self-control.
- When clients are highly reactive, use nondirective procedures to avoid arousing resistance.
- As clients proceed through therapy, their level of reactance may decrease. Then, it may be possible to employ more directive approaches and to offer more behavioral suggestions.

These recommendations have clear implications for working with the treatment-resistant client. Many of these clients, as previously discussed, are externalizing and highly reactive. These clients are not highly amenable to insight-oriented approaches, though it is possible to empathize with their emotional reactions to the here-and-now realities of their lives, specifically the coercive forces that have brought them into counseling. They are not likely to be ready to discuss their problems as defined by the referral source. They often do need a clear discussion about the consequences of different courses of action, if offered nonjudgmentally. That is, it is good to discuss what will happen to a probationer, for example, if he violates the terms of his probation. Yet, this discussion cannot be threatening, or else it will elicit reactive resistance. A discussion of consequences helps the client establish behavioral controls.

Other coerced clients may be cyclic clients who fluctuate between internalizing and externalizing. These clients are often diagnosed with borderline personality disorders (Lineham 1993) and are recognized by a pervasive pattern of instabilities of mood, interpersonal relationships, and self-image. They are often angry and suicidal, and they can be quite impulsive. They frequently make frantic efforts to avoid real or imagined abandonment.

Counselors may be tempted to use emotional arousal techniques when these clients are in a phase of internalization, but the danger is that the clients will quickly flip to become externalizing and will need behavioral controls. A controversial example of this is the treatment of sexually abused clients who are thought to have multiple personality disorders. Many therapists use cathartic techniques to surface the multiple personalities, but other therapists recommend cognitive techniques to help these clients maintain better emotional and behavioral control.

Rooney (1992) reviewed the research literature on work with involuntary clients and drew the following conclusions:

1. Court-ordered clients can achieve outcomes as successful as voluntary clients. Though research often does not distinguish between voluntary and involuntary clients or the various degrees and types of coercion, when such distinctions are made, there is little difference in outcome or satisfaction measures.

2. When the counselor attempts to help the client achieve what the client perceives as important, therapy is more effective. This "motivational congruence" can be enhanced by emphasizing choices and supporting the client's participation in goal selection.

3. Coercive interventions can produce results, but these results are time limited and do not extend beyond the time when the coercive pressure ends. The manipulation of the appearance of choice for clients, while with-holding actual choices, is questionably effective and may not be ethical. The use of punishment to suppress behavior seldom changes attitudes.

4. Clients are more likely to maintain a behavioral change if they can explain it as having occurred in their own best interest, rather than through the hope of gaining a reward or escaping a punishment.

Additional research on counseling treatment-resistant clients may reveal differences in outcome between coerced and voluntary clients in treatment; however, research techniques may not be sensitive enough to show the differences in various approaches. If Rooney is correct that coercion is counter-productive, then it would seem logical to believe that much treatment, which is coercion based, would be less effective than voluntary treatment provided for other problems.

Clearly, there are occasions that require the use of legitimate authority and power, but Rooney is correct that people seldom change permanently when forced, unless they somehow come to see the advantages of changing. This suggests the need for counselors to have a very clear idea of who their client is. Society may try to assign therapists the task of changing clients' behaviors in the interest of society at large, but counselors cannot be effective if they punish clients for misbehavior and try to make them change.

The responsibilities of the counselor toward society are set out in law. The law mandates when counselors must breach confidentiality, for example, and report child abuse or threats of harm to others. Employers, as well, may create dual responsibilities for a counselor. For example, probation officers have a clear responsibility to their employer, usually the state or local government, to provide protection to the public, while also serving in a helping capacity to probationers. It is, however, very difficult for counselors to be effective if they are more interested in satisfying the aims of an outside party than their client. This does not mean that a counselor should oblige clients who request assistance in remaining irresponsible; such a request is not in the client's interest even if he presently thinks so. However, the counselor's role is not to deliver the wrath of an angry society, no matter how morally justified that anger might be.

# Chapter 5

## Cynicism and Men in Therapy

$C$ynicism is an active mistrust of the intentions of others. It corrodes relationships and creates hostility. Cynicism is not mere skepticism nor perhaps as severe as paranoia, which by definition is without foundation. However, cynicism may be at the root of the wave of conspiracy theories developed to explain every event from the Kennedy assassination to the murder of Nicole Simpson.

Skepticism toward government is a healthy American tradition, but it would be a mistake to believe that cynicism toward government is unchanged from a decade or two ago. The rise in the popularity of the citizen militia movement is a testament to this. Polling data taken over the last several decades shows a clear and steady decline in the trust citizens have toward government (Kanter and Mirvis 1989). Their data show a clear trend toward cynicism in younger, poorly educated males in the workforce, though persons over age sixty-five and minorities show an alarming degree of mistrust and cynicism, as well, perhaps because of experiences in dealing with our government and society. Depending on how cynicism is defined, the data reveal that a majority of those polled now believe that government cannot be trusted to look out for the needs of ordinary people.

Many clients are cynical. This may be a reaction to changes in society or as a result of individual developmental issues. Clients who are cynical pose special problems in therapy. Cynical clients do not engage in therapy because they doubt that therapy can work. They doubt that the therapist is really interested in them or that they themselves are capable of making changes. Without the full participation of the client, counseling may not be effective, so something must be done to address the cynicism.

Cynics, unlike those with a paranoid personality, can point to a real basis for their feelings. Ample evidence supports some measure of doubt about the good intent of many of our fellow human beings. Cynics have lost a philosophical and spiritual compass to guide their life and provide it with a purpose. Without some sense of purpose in life, it is hard to develop feelings of involvement, trust, and respect for other human beings.

Freud thought that his patients were troubled by anxiety resulting from their inner conflicts, which stemmed from a clash between their instinctual drives and societal prohibitions. This explanation of psychological problems is the foundation for most psychotherapies.

Therapists today still deal with anxiety disorders, including panic attacks and phobias, but the counselor working with coerced clients sees fewer such clients. More and more clients are angry and blaming. The client who experiences anxiety typically "owns" the problem and seeks help for eliminating the symptom. The symptoms are ego dystonic, but techniques of psychotherapy that depend on the client being motivated to change do not work as well with the person who blames others.

Following the age of anxiety came the age of narcissism. Psychotherapy clients began to be variously described as having a distorted sense of self, grandiosity, and an inflated view of their entitlement. Lasch (1978) saw this narcissism as a result of a change in our society that resulted from a variety of factors, especially a decreased emphasis on the good of the social group and an increased emphasis on personal rights. Narcissistic people come into conflict with society because they manipulate relationships to their personal advantage and do not have a feeling of reciprocity essential for harmonious relationships. In Lasch's view, these are selfish people who reject the notion that there should be prohibitions and limitations on their wishes and desires. (These are the problems of entitlement discussed in chapter 2.)

In psychiatric nomenclature, difficult clients often are classified as having personality disorders: antisocial, borderline, or narcissistic, for example. (Though Lasch's conception of narcissism is somewhat different from a psychiatric definition, clarifying the difference is not essential for this discussion.) One of the difficulties with these diagnoses is that the definition of the problem is dependent on examining a web of social relationships and interpersonal boundaries and expectations, and this is difficult because society's norms and rules for behavior are rapidly changing.

It is somewhat easier to classify mental problems when the symptom resides within the person (as in panic) and the societal prohibitions are unquestioned than when the definition of the problem is a function of dysfunctional relationships and the expectations of normal behavior are in flux. For example, it is impossible to diagnose antisocial behavior without paying close attention to what is currently illegal. What is antisocial at one time may not be the next (drug use, for example), making therapy of personality disorders culturally relative.

Clients with personality disorders often are difficult to work with in counseling because their behavior is ego syntonic, that is, consistent with their views of right and wrong. Therefore, they see no reason to change and present little motivation to change in therapy. Whether or not the coerced client has a diagnosable personality disorder, there is a likelihood that he is in conflict with the authority who mandated therapy and with that authority's social expectations. The conflict may be relatively minor or may be significant and pervasive. In the latter case, it becomes more likely that the counselor will see the client as having antisocial characteristics.

We have now embarked on still a new era, perhaps the logical extension of the ages of anxiety and narcissism: the age of cynicism (Kanter and Mirvis 1989). Society has struggled to define standards for acceptable conduct and appropriate relationships. As these standards and boundaries in relationships shift over time, sometimes we are left feeling that all morals are culturally relative. Divorce, for example, once highly stigmatized now is almost a prerequisite for conducting marriage counseling! Our moral standards have been challenged to the point that it is difficult to say with certainty why anything is wrong.

Compounding the problem of accountability is the reality that our culture provides explanations to reduce the individual's ultimate responsibility for his own behavior. The social sciences have contributed to this process by showing that there are many genetic, cultural, and psychological variables that contribute to explaining behavior. The difficulty with this "psychologizing" of behavior is that it questions personal responsibility and gives the coerced client a tool with which to avoid self-scrutiny.

This "psychologizing" of behavior results in an uncertainty about moral standards and allows blaming of others when anything goes wrong. Everybody becomes a victim, but nobody seems to have any responsibility for what happens. Not only do those claiming victimhood feel mistreated and cynical, but those at whom the "victim's" finger is pointed also become cynical. The process of externalizing responsibility quickly leads to doubting or mistrusting others' motives and to a cynical view of people, generally.

Our society also has become cynical. We mistrust our government and leaders. They appear to be self-serving and to lie to us without being accountable. We mistrust our churches because some of their leaders preach one message and live another. Hypocrisy engenders cynical responses. While searching for personal values and meaning, individuals feel frustrated because there is no believable universal philosophy that explains the meaning of life in a reliable way .

Science has taken away simplistic explanations of creation and morality and has left cultural relativism, the view that values are not universal but are created by each culture. And if the culture defines morality, then whatever the culture permits is acceptable. It is only a short step then for the individual to dismiss the cultural norms as irrelevant to himself, thereby permitting an individual to define his own morality based on whatever is good for himself. Thus, the "I want what I want when I want it" mode of thinking becomes operational.

Without a belief in something larger and more enduring than ourselves, without a touchstone to anchor our conduct in principle, there is nothing to counter the "me-first" attitudes of those who decline to contribute to the common good. When it appears that others act only out of self-interest, the feeling of belonging to a caring society falls and cynicism rises.

In a culture where many special interest groups feel victimized and entitled to special rights and protections, the broader culture develops compassion burnout and cynicism as the willingness of "victims" to take responsibility for themselves is questioned. Society has become complex and fragmented, and it is difficult to take time to try to understand the points of view of all the groups who claim to be disadvantaged. Only the stories of the most obviously innocent victims can be quickly and efficiently portrayed in the media. The more complex problems take too much time for many people to understand. Counselors have a special responsibility to take the time to understand their client's social, economic, and cultural background. Counselors who wish to make a difference should become familiar with the multicultural material from the mental health field.

Society wants to respond with punishment to people who lash out in anger to their perceived oppression, but we feel conflicted over the use of punishment (Menninger 1968). As therapists, we may feel sympathy for the anxious person, but we also may become defensive when we are blamed and accused of not having met the needs of the many groups of people who feel taken advantage of in society. Criminals excuse their behavior by rejecting and blaming society, and the rest of us wonder where their sense of personal responsibility has gone. As people have abandoned anxiety in favor of anger and blame, cynicism has developed as a backlash.

A difficulty with these developments is that there is truth in the claims of the victims. Battered women (and men), African-Americans, victims of sexual abuse, and others have been harmed at the hands of society. Most inmates also could claim that they were victims of an unjust society. It is difficult to determine when to allow people not to be accountable for themselves because of circumstances outside their control. When we see people making excuses, we become cynical, but how do we decide whose claims of nonresponsibility are justified? Despite these claims, we can help our clients grow and develop approaches that will make them better off than they have been.

Affected by the nihilism of our time, many therapists approach therapy simplistically and look for magical techniques but do not really believe they exist. They doubt that therapy is useful because it does not provide answers to what is morally right and wrong. (Is the recent emphasis on brief therapy an admission that we cannot help clients with the complicated task of developing deeper personal meaning in their lives because we do not have it in our own?) We have difficulty explaining to our clients why they should respect the law when it is clear that crime often does pay and pays well if done well.

Therapists may become nihilistic, as well, because they know they cannot fix the major societal problems that beset clients. With many clients, the enormous problems that would need to be fixed in their environments seems just too overwhelming to tackle, and therapy seems pointless if we do not. Yet, overcoming our own cynicism and realizing that some changes are possible may lead to other changes both in our clients and in society. By keeping hope alive, we can do more than we expect on our most cynical days.

Glasser's Reality Therapy (1965) encouraged therapists to take a position with clients about moral issues, but it does not provide clear answers to specific questions about morality. Glasser is right that therapists must have a moral perspective not only to be effective but to avoid cynicism. The difficulty is that it is hard to have moral positions without being moralistic. This book certainly does not have the answer to our nation's growing cynicism, but it is important to raise our consciousness about the effects of cynicism on the therapy process and to offer some beginning suggestions for what we can do about it.

In many ways, cynicism seems to be a reaction to social issues: hypocrisy in institutions, changes in social norms, the fall of religious systems, and beliefs that are cast into doubt by scientific exploration, but there are psychological causes of cynicism, as well. Cynicism is people's reaction to perceptions that they have been lied to or deceived by parents or important authority figures. This, in turn, creates a mistrust in people, in language, and in the capacity of people to work out problems together. In a psychological sense, the person struggling with cynicism has not mastered the early developmental stage of establishing trust in others. The person also may not trust himself and, consequently, projects his mistrust onto others.

Therapists may be more comfortable working with cynicism at the personal/psychological level rather than societal level because solutions may be less controversial and more manageable. While therapists may not be able to change racism or poverty, they can help clients discuss betrayal by parents and other authority figures.

Cynicism may be perceived as a defense mechanism, perhaps to ward off depression. While a depressed person feels hopeless, the cynical person has only given up hope that others can be trusted to have good intent. The cynical person relies on himself, and though this may be lonely, it is better than being depressed. Of course, this has major implications for therapy because the client's willingness to engage in therapy is compromised by his cynical mistrust of the therapist's intentions. Cynical clients are afraid that people—including the therapist—cannot be trusted, but they also are afraid to become depressed: to admit that they need the help of someone else. They, then, worry about confirming their belief that the person who provides that help is untrustworthy.

One clear implication of this view of cynicism is that therapists must be very consistent in word and deed. If a promise is made, it must be kept; otherwise, the client confirms again that people, including the therapist, cannot be trusted to do what they say they will do. Many clients, especially in prison settings, set up specific tests to see whether they can trust therapists, but most clients are probably doing checks at one level of consciousness or another. This is certainly Weiss' view, as discussed earlier. At an observational level, it seems apparent that clients are verifying their beliefs if not hoping to disconfirm their more dysfunctional views.

The more cynical the client is, the more important it becomes to address the issue of trust in the relationship. Doing this directly is often awkward. However, the same issue can be approached by asking clients about their trust of people, generally, and their confidence in being able to talk through problems. Eventually, the therapist can directly touch on the client's confidence (or lack of confidence) in the therapist and the therapy process. Once some degree of mistrust and cynicism is labeled and acknowledged, it is possible then to "depth-dive" by asking the client to recount other times in his life when he has had this feeling of mistrust (Heitler 1993).

This historical review allows the therapist to examine the client's development and provides insight into the client's character. Before clients can use counseling to solve other major life problems, they must first overcome their cynical mistrust of counseling as an exchange of untrustworthy language and their mistrust of the counselor as another person who will not do what was promised or who will eventually betray their confidences. Once again, the major resistances in counseling are the client's resistance to counseling, change, and the counselor.

## Cynicism and Men's Issues

Men, perhaps more than women, mistrust language and relationships, and they, therefore, decline to use language to process conflict. This is perhaps why men are often accused by women of not talking about their feelings. It is not that men do not have feelings; rather, they are less inclined, or perhaps less able, to discuss them (Osherson 1992; Twohey and Ewing 1995). Why do men mistrust language and relationships? Why are they unable to articulate what their concerns are? Answering these questions requires some examination of the social and psychological environment in which men are raised.

To begin, physical violence rather than verbal problem solving has become accepted as a normal way of life for men. Biracree (1988) noted that more than 40,000 people per year are killed on television shows. Ninety-seven percent of those murdered on television are men. According to Biracree's data, about 95 percent of the people killed in movies are men.

Outside of the media, the real statistics are just as alarming. Farrell (1993) reported that males occupy over 90 percent of twenty-four of the top twenty-five most dangerous jobs in the country. Every hour of every workday, a construction worker (almost always male) loses his life in a construction accident. Men are twice as likely as women to be victims of a violent offense and three times as likely to be a victim of a homicide. Friedman (1993) reported that in 1990 there were 23,000 homicides, of which more than 17,000 were men.

Women commit approximately 1,900 (under 10 percent) of the homicides each year, but 90 percent of their victims are men (Humphrey 1989). The facts of domestic violence reveal that women commit violence against men as frequently as men aggress against women (Straus and Gelles 1986; Harris 1987). Yet, since 1977 only one woman has been executed (Bureau of Justice Statistics 1993). The grim facts may be more easily understood by examining two rather typical years. For example, in 1993, 1,004 men were murdered by women, 335 of whom were husbands killed by their wives, and in 1988, 1,123 men were killed by women, 476 of whom were married to the woman who killed them (Uniform Crime Report 1993, 1988). Clearly, men commit the bulk of violent crimes, but they commit them primarily against other men, as do women.

These data may be incomprehensible and startling to the reader. The average man has not begun to integrate the meaning of these facts into his life. As yet, he has displayed little conscious rage that his life expectancy is seven years less than that of the average woman. As Farrell pointed out, both white women and black women have longer life expectancies than white men and black men. Men have higher rates of cardiovascular disease and other stress-related disorders than women, yet money for health research is disproportionately directed at women's health issues such as breast cancer, when equally devastating male health problems such as prostate cancer receive substantially less funding (Farrell 1993).

What the average male does know is that society expects him to behave in a prescribed manner. At a cultural level, boys are encouraged to be independent and are teased if they are not. Boys learn that if they cry, they will be called sissies and experience shame in relationships if they feel dependency or express their emotions. Men may express their feelings more through their behavior than women, and men are socialized to express anger when they are hurt. Tannen (1994) explained how women are socialized to develop relationships and develop rapport with others, while men are trained to achieve competitive advantage. Working for this competitive advantage cuts men off from friendships and the comfort of social supports. They lose outlets for expression and become emotionally isolated.

Despite recent calls from feminists for men to get in touch with their feelings, men sense a great risk in doing so in public. Farrell (1983) argued that men are socialized to compete, achieve, acquire, and protect in order to attract, marry, and provide for women and families. There is little room for the "weak" male. Unfortunately, many men cannot compete, and the results are endemic. Males commit suicide at a rate of two to six times that of women at ages nine through twenty-five (Farrell 1993). The suicide rate suggests that men are unable to unravel the binds they experience.

Certainly, there are numerous legitimate empowerment issues confronting women in this society. Women are the major users of psychotherapy on a voluntary basis, and this suggests that men do not perceive a need to seek out help or negatively perceive the help that is available. Erickson (1993) explained her belief that loss is what brings most people into psychotherapy, but men seek out therapy less often than women because they are socialized against the expression of any emotion but anger. The data are clear, however, that many men are in deep trouble, whether they perceive it or not.

Farrell referred to men as the "expendable sex" because the male role is to provide for the women and children at personal risk and expense. At some level, many men recognize that they are devalued in society if they are unable or unwilling to assume the expected role. Some respond by assuming the role and the responsibilities if they can. Other men fail or refuse the responsibilities. Thus, men tend either to be highly successful or, in the alternative, failures. Men occupy the majority of leadership positions in society, but they also occupy most of the prison beds.

Many men who try to conform to expectations and "do the right thing" at some time begin to question their roles and become cynical. Men who went to Vietnam to serve their country came home to rejection. They did what they were asked to do. Then, they were branded as killers. Lawson (1995) explored the difficulties faced by veterans in re-establishing trust after traumatic war experiences and noted that the process is particularly difficult for men whose early childhood experiences had not provided a core basis for feeling trust. In the 1990s, men have worked hard to succeed in their careers but now are branded as oppressors. It is little wonder that they are often cynical.

It is not possible to deal with treatment resistance in men without having some appreciation for the binds that society places on men, especially about discussing their feelings in a culture that claims to value sensitivity but often rewards aggressiveness with attention and approval. Try to visualize a teenage boy weeping publicly over the death of a pet. Now, visualize a teenage girl crying over the pet's death. If these events seem equally likely, then perhaps our society has advanced in allowing both sexes to express emotion. It seems probable though that the boy would deny his pain. He might express an irrational or misdirected anger, or pretend he is just not upset. Even if he feels the loss and experiences the grief, he cries alone.

The counselor who wants to work with treatment-resistant clients, who are often men, must develop an understanding of men's issues and of the cynicism that many men carry. This is surely not work for brief therapy. Erickson (1993) has provided a comprehensive text for women who want to counsel men. Other works on understanding men (Osherson 1992; Farrell 1993) are strongly recommended reading, as well. Welo's workbook *Life Beyond Loss* (1994) deals with issues of grief and loss that often lead to life problems when left unresolved.

# Chapter 6

# *Legal and Ethical Issues in Counseling Involuntary Clients*

*T*his chapter includes a discussion of the ethical issues related to counseling treatment-resistant clients, including the right to refuse treatment; the right to informed consent, confidentiality, and privileged communication; and the counselor's obligation to offer treatment to clients who, at times, may initially decline. The reader may wish to explore general readings on ethics in the criminal justice system (Monahan 1980; Rooney 1992) and counseling, in general (Van Hoose and Kottler 1985; Young 1992; Nugent 1994).

Some counseling texts assert that the counseling relationship can only occur with the mutual consent of both the client and the counselor (Shertzer and Stone 1974; Patterson 1980; Young 1992). This is perhaps the ideal relationship, but it is not often found in many contexts, including corrections, substance abuse counseling, and even marital and family therapy (see Fox 1980 and McCarthy 1984 for an introduction to correctional issues). Nugent (1994) said that counseling could occur with involuntary clients if there were a reason to believe that the client was in imminent danger, but many, perhaps most, clients involuntarily in counseling are not in imminent danger. Some acceptable compromise must be explored to ethically authorize offering assistance to these clients.

As previously discussed, some form of coercion is present in most counseling situations. Though clients may not be formally mandated to undergo counseling, some type of pressure has been exerted to get the client to counseling; therefore, the counseling is not, strictly speaking, voluntary. It is an error in reasoning to believe that the client is attending either voluntarily or involuntarily. Therefore, when considering ethical issues, some consideration must be given to the degree of pressure and submission to pressure that has occurred to bring the client into treatment.

In the most extreme case, a client may be incarcerated and expected to attend treatment (Kramer 1985; Geiser and Annitto 1985). Coerced treatment in institutions can lead to violence (Lion and Reid 1985). Clearly, the counselor must consider the client's legal right to refuse treatment and the client's right to informed consent about the nature of the treatment being offered (Rooney 1992). Clients have a right to treatment and may be required to receive treatment when they present a clear and present danger to themselves or others (Kittrie 1971; Bernbaum 1960). The courts have clearly ruled that the presence of mental illness alone is not sufficient to require treatment.

If a client steadfastly refuses to participate in therapy, practically speaking, there usually is not much of a legal issue with regard to forcing the person into treatment. It is not possible to force clients to talk absent holding a gun to their heads. Few counselors have enough leverage or threats to be considered truly coercive, and if clients can be talked into talking, the issue of illegally coerced treatment is probably moot. An exception to this is treatment in the prison setting, in which prisoners may volunteer to submit to extreme therapies in hopes of obtaining early release. The courts have prohibited the use of many extreme treatments in such settings on the assumption that no one is truly free to volunteer in such settings because the environment is inherently coercive.

The right to refuse treatment, such as medication, generally becomes an issue in involuntary commitment. State commitment laws vary. Therapists who work in psychiatric or correctional settings should consult with legal counsel for their facility about accepted procedures. Forced participation in medical procedures, including psychosurgery, is now unlawful in most cases.

From an ethical perspective, it may be helpful for the counselor to think about preliminary discussions with the client about whether to participate in counseling as preparation for the counseling rather than as treatment. How can there be anything unethical about discussing the pros and cons of participating in treatment? Through discussion, the client may be more willing to participate. In a sense, beginning work with a counseling-resistant client involves selling the client on therapy rather than doing therapy. There is no legal right in the United States to avoid salespeople! Again, as a practical matter, if a counselor tries to explain counseling to the client and the client steadfastly refuses to talk about it, there is not much point in persisting, regardless of whether persisting is ethical.

On the other hand, there is an ethical case to be made for trying very hard to persuade clients to enter into treatment when it is apparent that the client eventually will be at risk without treatment. For example, parents of a teenage boy bring him to counseling against his will. They are concerned about his drug use. The boy clearly states that he does not want to come to counseling, yet just as clearly he reveals an anxiety about his life. The boy rejects counseling on the surface, perhaps because he cannot consciously "choose" to work on his problems. It also is apparent that his drug use is not in his best interest. Clearly, the parents have a legal right to get treatment for their child, but is it ethical to treat the boy who does not want to participate?

On the other hand, is it ethical to dismiss the boy as "unwilling" to undergo treatment because that is how he says he feels? The most ethical thing to do may be to try to talk the boy into participating. At some point, he must have some willingness to participate for the counseling to do any good, and it is in his interest ultimately to examine his problem. It may be paternalistic for counselors to believe that they know what is best for a client, but sometimes that judgment must be made, thoughtfully and carefully. Client autonomy and self-direction are the ultimate aims of any treatment, and therapists must be careful not to compromise these aims. Then, as long as interventions are chosen for the client's interests, not the counselor's, it is unlikely that the counselor's paternalism will outweigh the benefits of treatment.

Some evidence, however, shows that forced treatment can do

harm, even if it is well-intentioned treatment. A report by the National Institute for Juvenile Justice and Delinquency Protection (1983) showed that forced treatment was a precursor to violence in juvenile institutions and that voluntary choice was necessary to encourage clients to take ownership in their therapeutic program (Lion and Reed 1985). It is important, however, not to expect troubled clients to enthusiastically endorse treatment. Counselors should expect to have to go slowly to gain the cooperation necessary for effective treatment.

Just as clients ultimately have the right to refuse treatment, counselors have the right and the responsibility not to offer inadequate and insufficient treatment. A client who is difficult to engage in treatment may require many sessions before a reasonable working alliance can be established. A personality-disordered client is not likely to be effectively treated with brief therapy. Recognizing this, the counselor should consider not accepting clients whose problems require intensive therapy but whose insurance will not allow more than a few sessions. It may be possible to get mutual agreement on very small goals, but there should be no pretense of fixing lifelong problems in such a short time. Many clients need intensive, frequent sessions to begin their work, and if their insurance will pay for only one session per week, as is often the case, the therapist must make some arrangement for providing the necessary intensity. In some cases, the insurance company may agree to provide coverage for intensive outpatient therapy in lieu of hospitalization, but without such an agreement, the therapist may not be reimbursed for extra sessions. It is not acceptable to allow the client to accumulate a huge debt for therapy, because these debts themselves can become a source of resentment for the provider and client alike, and become an impediment to future work.

It is better not to begin the treatment than to abandon the client when financial compensation runs out after a few weeks. Clarifying the requirements of treatment with the insurance carrier or third-party payer after an initial diagnostic session may help get a commitment for the level and intensity of the work needed. Therapists working for agencies or institutions should clarify with supervisors what level of treatment is needed and secure a commitment for adequate time and resources before undertaking therapy. If such commitment is not available, the client may be referred to a community mental health center or other public agency that may have external funding to help offset expenses for clients who cannot pay. Referral to university programs in which students provide free therapy at first may appear to be an ethical alternative but, in reality, may only provide a rationalization for not seeing a difficult client. These programs probably will not offer long-term therapy because the students tend to graduate and move away and probably are not ready to treat such difficult cases anyway.

# Confidentiality and Privileged Communication

In all cases, treatment-resistant clients have the same rights to confidentiality as any other client would have. However, it would be naive to pretend that the coerced client is no different from other clients in the counseling relationship. Whether the client is extremely or only somewhat resistant, whenever there is external pressure for counseling, the counselor is under pressure to divulge information about the counseling to third parties. Especially in institutional work, the counselor may have divided loyalty between the employer and the client (Berman and Segal 1982). The American Psychological Association's report on ethics of psychologists in the criminal justice system addressed some of these issues and maintained that the therapist's primary responsibility is to the client (American Psychological Association 1978). Newer codes of ethics by the American Board of Forensic Psychologists (1993) also provide some guidance for psychologists who perform in this arena.

At the practice level, however, the therapist will face a great deal of pressure to provide information to courts and employers, ostensibly, for the purpose of protecting the public or advancing societal interests. Clear examples of the limits of confidentiality include reports of child abuse. Threats of harm to others also are a cause for breaching confidentiality in most cases since the *Tarasoff* case (see Costa and Altekruse 1994, for a thorough discussion of duty-to-warn issues).

Therapists who function as part of a treatment team will need to assess what aspects of the individual counseling relationship will be shared with the team and which information will be kept confidential. There is no easy solution to this problem. Therapists who ascribe to certain models of therapy, perhaps psychodynamic theories, may believe that the therapy relationship should be sacrosanct. Other therapists, for example family therapists, may be more inclined to see such strict boundaries as inviting collusion and inappropriate secrets. At a minimum, therapists need to clarify to themselves and with the client what communications will be kept strictly confidential.

State laws differ on the legal protections clients have to privileged communication with various types of therapists. Privileged communication refers to the client's legal right to ask the counselor not to divulge information to courts through the subpoena process. Clients seeing unlicensed practitioners often have no protection, and it is up to the counselor to try to follow ethical, not legal, guidelines of confidentiality. At a minimum, clients should be informed of what protections they do and do not have in the counseling relationship. Psychologists, social workers, mental health counselors, and psychiatrists are treated differently by law in many jurisdictions, so it is up to individual therapists to understand the law in their own state and practice setting.

Clients have the right to due process before they can be deprived of life, liberty, or property (Rooney 1992). There are few counseling situations in which the counselor has the authority to deprive a client of these rights. However, in institutional work, counselors often do participate in treatment teams that make decisions or recommendations that affect the client's life. Probation and parole officers, likewise, make such important decisions, and due process considerations are important. It is always wise to have a written description of procedures that are used to make any decision that materially affects a client, including the right to appeal. Arbitrary and capricious decisions often violate due process and, in addition, destroy the client's sense of trust and fair play.

## Record Keeping Requirements

Legal and ethical requirements for record keeping are becoming increasingly stringent. Most ethical guidelines call for keeping a statement of the problem, history of past treatments, diagnosis, treatment plan, and notes of sessions, in addition to dates of treatment and fee agreements. Therapists who do not keep such records put themselves at some risk; nevertheless, the presence of such records invites subpoenas when third parties want information about the client.

Therapists should understand that a subpoena to produce documents is merely a lawyer's request, not an order of the court. It is not wise to release information to anyone until the client has signed a release or until a clear order has been issued by a judge. In many cases, when a court requires information, a request can be made to disclose the information in a judge's chambers to keep information from becoming public. It is probably a good idea in any questionable incident to get an attorney's opinion about the risk of releasing files.

Therapists should never delete information from files after they receive a subpoena, nor should they alter any information. Keeping two files, one clinical file and one official file, is also not acceptable in most states. Even when making initial notes, if a mistake is made, it is not wise to erase or blot out the mistake because if records are later subpoenaed, it will appear that the records have been altered. It is better just to draw a line through any errors and then proceed to rewrite the note.

Many health insurance companies require detailed treatment plans, including much sensitive information about the client, before approving payment. Therapists may try to limit the information disclosed to insurance companies, but clients give tacit approval for such disclosure when they ask that charges be submitted to insurance. (Even so, it is usually better to get an official release signed by the client.) Disclosure to insurance companies becomes especially important with clients who have legal problems and who may be reluctant to be in treatment in the first place. Many insurance companies will not pay for court-ordered treatment or treatment that became necessary because of a legal violation. For example, insurance will not usually pay for treatment of a rapist, even if a *DSM-IV* diagnosis is applicable. Insurance policies vary, but it is important not to mislead the insurance company just to get payment approved. Yet, clients often become even more resistant to treatment when they have to pay therapy fees out of pocket, but that is not the insurance company's problem; it is the client's.

## Ethical Considerations for Counseling Interventions

Another issue to consider in working with involuntary clients is the extent to which counselors should manipulate and persuade their clients. Are some techniques too "hard sell" or "too tricky"? How much anxiety or emotional pain should counselors be allowed to arouse through confrontation?

The ends do not always justify the means. It is hard to question the ethics of providing information to a client, and withholding information may well be unethical. Providing information about consequences, agency rules, community resources, drug effects, and so on is not likely to provoke much controversy. However, failure to tell a client about limits to confidentiality is almost certainly unethical, even if the client might become reticent to talk when so informed.

Another intervention unlikely to be questioned is active listening. Basic responding skills in counseling help the client explore options and choices, even if the client does not fully understand the counselor's intent to help in this way. The effectiveness of other interventions, such as paradoxical directives, may be compromised if their purpose is explained in advance to the client, yet failure to explain these procedures to the client may violate the principle of timely and informed consent, which requires that the client have understandable explanations of procedures at an appropriate time.

Erickson (1980) noted that many powerful techniques eventually boomerang if they are done primarily for the therapist's benefit rather than for the client's. The ethics of most interventions turn on the question of who benefits. Erickson believed that people resented being manipulated if they had been conned into doing something that did not benefit them, but they were not resentful if they were tricked into behavior that helped them in the long run. Counselors must choose for themselves whether techniques are justified. They should base their decisions on accurate knowledge of probable benefits to the client as well as on a consideration of their own motives for wanting the client to change.

The mere fact that an intervention is unpleasant does not make it unethical. Criminals must feel pain, uncertainty, anxiety, and even self-disgust to undergo change (Samenow 1984; Korn and McCorkle 1959). Almost any powerful technique can create pain, but the length of that pain and the benefit it carries are the key considerations in whether to induce it. Short-term pain may be necessary for long-term gain.

Though the ethical permissibility of different interventions may be on a continuum, there is no guarantee that the most effective procedure will always be the most ethical. The more powerful the technique, the more potential for harm to the client, and therefore, the more likely the technique could be used unethically. Aversive conditioning may be powerful, but if imposed on clients against their will, it is very questionable in almost all circumstances. It is always wise to submit any risky procedure to an ethics review panel for approval before proceeding.

Some basic recommendations regarding ethical considerations include the following:

1. Counselors should know the law of their state and the codes of ethics of their mental health discipline. They should understand the expectations of the agency for whom they work and discuss with their supervisors or administrators potential conflicts of the agency's expectations with laws and ethical codes. If an agency expects the counselor to freely share information with legal authorities without explicit comments from the client, compliance with such an expectation places the counselor in serious jeopardy.

2. Clients should always be advised in advance about limits to confidentiality and privileged communication. Counselors should explain privileged communication to clients who may be in conflict with the legal system.

3. Therapists should keep thorough and complete records and should not try to alter records to delete information that clients may not want revealed through a subpoena or court order. Obtain a client's written consent before releasing information, whenever possible.

4. Clients should understand their treatment. Clients should give timely and informed consent. It is difficult to justify paradoxical interventions in many cases because it is countertherapeutic to explain the treatment in advance to the client. Timely and informed consent must occur prior to any intervention, even before paradoxical interventions.

5. Counselors who deal with involuntary commitments should work closely with legal counsel for their facility to understand the laws of their state and the policies and procedures of their institution. Medication may be imposed on clients following legal guidelines and, of course, after it is prescribed by a physician.

6. When a counselor's decisions have a material impact on a client in a treatment setting, due process considerations are present. No client should be deprived of liberty or property without clear, written procedures, and there should be a clear appeal process that is explained to the client.

In the final analysis, reasonable efforts to persuade a reluctant client to participate in counseling are humanitarian and ethical. It is not unethical to try to help clients see what is in their best interest through reasoning and rapport building. The assumption that clients must be motivated to participate before counseling can begin is simplistic. It ignores the reality of a complex world in which clients are motivated by many things to greater and lesser degrees, and it ignores the reality that it is sometimes unethical *not* to try to convince people to become clients.

# Chapter 7

*Counseling*
*Antisocial*
*Clients*

$C$ounseling clients with deeply ingrained criminal tendencies is a difficult task, and true attitudinal and long-lasting behavioral change may not be possible in many, if not most, cases. The counselor should keep in mind that the majority of involuntary clients will have a history of conflicted relationships and behaviors that may qualify as antisocial. Samenow (1976) argued that irresponsible conduct is on a continuum from mild to severe. Yet, not everyone who has committed an irresponsible act is antisocial or "criminal." Counselors should keep the concept of the continuum in mind when making diagnoses.

The diagnosis of an antisocial personality disorder in the *DSM-IV* (1994) generally requires a pattern of irresponsible behavior, including difficulties with work, social norms, parenting, and relationships; aggressiveness; lying; recklessness; and disregard for the safety of others. Antisocial personalities do not learn from the consequences of their behavior, perhaps because an intense stimulus or consequence is needed to get the person's attention. The reason an antisocial personality seeks high-intensity activities may indeed stem from the difficulty of attaining emotional arousal through low-intensity stimulation.

The most significant aspect of the treatment of the antisocial personality is this individual's difficulty with attachment and bonding. Most people in relationships develop a sense of reciprocity and mutual obligation. In counseling, antisocial personalities do not develop a sense of connection to the therapist or a desire to please or conform to expectations. Since much of the research on therapy effectiveness points to the importance of the development of a therapeutic alliance, we can understand why counseling with antisocial personalities is often limited to factual, practical explorations of the probable consequences of various behaviors. The antisocial person does not internalize the counselor's values or care what the counselor thinks. Additionally, the antisocial person does not see a reason to change because of principles or moral imperatives.

In clinical practice, differential diagnosis of various personality disorders, including narcissistic and borderline disorders, is unreliable. Treatment setting may dictate diagnosis as much as client symptoms or behavior. Factors such as race and socioeconomic group may affect which treatment setting is made available to the client (Harris and Kirk 1983; Harris 1984). Thus, the counselor who is attempting to select an appropriate treatment approach is in a quandary. The truly antisocial client may try to manipulate the counselor who attempts to be empathetic. Clients who are not antisocial need a more empathetic approach to overcome their hostility toward the therapy. There is no substitute for clinical judgment and intuitive feelings here.

The counselor should follow Samenow's (1984) admonition to be neither cynical nor gullible in therapy with the antisocial client, but there is no absolute formula to follow to avoid these traps. It is possible to be friendly with all clients, though to be cordial with antisocial clients may be a more apt descriptor and recommendation. In institutional settings, it can be very helpful to be completely clear about rules and procedures and follow them closely with all clients. In therapy, counselors should be very clear about ethical guidelines and have clear ideas about what the therapeutic relationship is and is not. If a counselor has followed all agency and ethical guidelines and attempts to be empathetic with an antisocial client, the counselor's efforts may have been wasted, but these steps will not have created danger.

If comprehensive and thorough clinical information has preceded the client, the counselor can probably make a reasonable preliminary assessment of the client's character structure, though it is wise not to get locked into a view before meeting the client. If there is no referral information, proceed slowly and attempt to assess the client during the first session or two. Counselors should be extremely wary of making any self-disclosures until the client has been adequately assessed. In most therapies, significant self-disclosure should be very limited until the latter stages of the process.

Experts recommend using cognitive approaches with a wide range of personality-disordered clients, especially antisocial personalities. The literature on offender populations emphasizes similarities in thought processes among various types of offenders. A brief review of some literature on various types of offenders will highlight these concepts.

Cressey's (1953) study of embezzlers showed their use of cognitive neutralization techniques to deny responsibility for their acts. Neutralization techniques deny that there is a victim, an injury, or personal blame. The embezzler commonly referred to embezzlement as "borrowing," a cognitive strategy that demonstrates loss to the "lender."

Neutralization techniques are necessary only for persons whose basic values are prosocial. Offenders who have internalized antisocial values have no need to excuse their behavior to protect their self-concept (Green 1990). Furthermore, neutralization is different from rationalization, which follows rather than precedes the criminal act. Rationalization is an automatic and unconscious repression designed to deal with guilt (Green 1990).

Five neutralization techniques used most frequently by juvenile offenders include: denial of the victim; denial of the injury; denial of responsibility; condemnation of condemners; and appeals to higher loyalties (Sykes and Matza 1957). Minor (1981) added two more neutralizations: necessity (I need the proceeds of this crime); and the metaphor of the ledger (I only do this occasionally).

The cognitive processes used by the Watergate criminals to explain their crimes included: authorization (someone higher up approved), routinization (this is just the way it has always been done), and dehumanization (those who were affected by our acts are less important than other people) (Smith and Berlin 1988). Charny (1982) noted essentially the same mental processes in Nazi war criminals and other perpetrators of genocide at various times in history.

White-collar offenders use cognitive strategies in their efforts to deny guilt, minimize the seriousness of their rule breaking, and retain a view of themselves as "good" people (Benson 1985). Walters (1990) remarked that Benson's findings were remarkably similar to those of Yochelson and Samenow (1976), who studied offenders adjudicated not guilty by reason of insanity after committing serious crimes against property and person. Yochelson and Samenow's and Walters' research is discussed in more detail later. These various authors identify very similar thought processes in the offender populations. This, in turn, may point logically to cognitive approaches in the treatment of offenders with "irresponsible" thinking, if not outright antisocial personalities.

Different counseling approaches may be needed for offenders at various stages in their criminal behavior. Stewart (1992) described counseling approaches with first-time offenders, offenders developing a criminal lifestyle, and criminals who have been maintaining criminal lifestyles. With earlier-stage offenders, he argued, it may still be possible to use the counseling relationship as a vehicle to bring about change, but that for the established offender it is important to concentrate on cognitive and behavioral change. This is consistent with the recommendations of Beutler and Consoli (1992). Their research shows the effectiveness of cognitive self-control strategies, especially for clients with cyclic (borderline, narcissistic) tendencies.

We may examine behavior by looking at the primary source from which the person gains satisfaction and then seeing how the person attempts to avoid pain and distress (Millon and Klerman 1986). This theory provides a way to understand the antisocial personality and how clients with it may be resistant to treatment.

According to this theory, there are five categories of individual clients of this type. First, there are the detached people who experience few rewards either from themselves or others. The second category, the discordant personalities, are persons who experience pain as pleasure or pleasure as pain. The third category, the dependent personalities, includes those who gauge their satisfaction or discomfort by how others feel about them. The fourth category, the independent, is the person whose gratification is self-determined. Finally, people who are in conflict about whether to be self-guided or guided by others are referred to as ambivalent.

Clearly, a person who is detached from others and gains little reward from self or others is difficult to motivate in therapy because this person perceives no gain from participating. Clients who are discordant are difficult to understand; their responses are counter intuitive to the thinking of the therapist. These clients often appear self-destructive and are difficult to motivate with socially acceptable reinforcers. The dependent person may lean too much on the therapist and depend too much on the therapist's opinion rather than form a distinct opinion and assume responsibility for it. The independent personality in its extreme form is unresponsive to the therapeutic relationship, and the person does not care what the therapist thinks. The ambivalent person may shift cyclically between being self- and therapist-guided, creating confusion and disarray in the counseling process.

Each of these types of personalities chooses a coping behavior to maximize reward and minimize pain. These coping behaviors are either active or passive. Active persons achieve gratification by intervening and manipulating life events while passive persons are restrained, resigned, and yielding.

Combining the two dimensions and types of personalities and active or passive orientation creates ten basic personality styles, though more styles are created by considering extremes of the combinations. We will simplify the theory to discuss its implications.

Of special interest in this theory is the personality created by the combination of an independent personality with an active-coping mechanism. This is the antisocial personality. Forging a therapeutic relationship with people of this nature will be difficult because of their lack of interest in receiving reinforcement from other persons, including therapists. In its extreme form, people with this personality have little regard for others and actively seek to gratify themselves, even at the expense of others.

In contrast to the dependent personality, people with an independent personality value the opinion of the therapist only for the utilitarian value it may have. For example, the independent client would not follow a therapist's suggestion to please the therapist, but he might do so if the suggestion seemed to have the potential for bringing him material gain.

Further description of the active, independent (antisocial) personality style, theoretically explained by Millon, is provided by Walters and White (1989), who synthesized the work of several cognitive therapies, including that of Ellis and Yochelson and Samenow. They identified eight cognitive patterns offenders use in maintaining a criminal lifestyle, and they offered basic suggestions for therapy interventions. The cognitive patterns include the following:

**Mollification.** Offenders blame their criminal behavior on social injustices, circumstances, or victims. They minimize their own criminal behavior.

**Cutoff.** Conscious actions on the part of offenders prevent them from thinking about the consequences of their behavior to eliminate fears that could make the offender hesitate or stop. For example, some offenders intentionally use drugs to create a sense of invulnerability and to block feelings of fear before they commit a crime.

**Entitlement.** Offenders feel that they have the right to the property of others. They believe they are so special that the rules of society do not apply to them. Their wants are confused with their needs.

**Power orientation.** Offenders feel they must have control over others, especially when they are feeling vulnerable.

**Sentimentality.** In this behavior pattern, repeat offenders express tender feelings and normalcy, even though most of their behaviors are deviant and destructive. For example, an inmate may become quite sentimental about his mother, though he has hurt her many times.

**Super optimism.** This is the feeling that offenders can achieve anything, no matter how improbable.

**Cognitive indolence.** In this thinking pattern, repeat offenders do not work hard at thinking things through. They take the easy way out.

**Fragmentation.** Offenders do not stick with a line of thinking or commitment to others. They forget their goals or carelessly replace them by other interests.

Treatment of individuals with these cognitive patterns begins with a thorough assessment of their criminal lifestyle and the probable cognitions associated with their criminal behavior. Yochelson and Samenow (1976, 1977) recommended confronting the offender with the three basic choices: to change, to kill oneself, or to not change and thus to continue in a criminal lifestyle with the attendant consequences. If an offender is tired of the consequences of a criminal lifestyle (being arrested, serving time, and so on), then he can examine his underlying irresponsible cognitions and begin to change them. In this approach, the assumption is that the client chooses the criminal behavior and that there is little need to understand "causes" of the criminal thinking. The therapy is aimed at changing cognitions.

The change process for cognitions requires in-depth recording of moment-to-moment thoughts and labeling of these thoughts, according to cognitive pattern. Using a variety of cognitive therapy techniques, the counselor challenges the offender's basic cognitions. For example, the pattern of cognitive indolence is attacked by challenging the criminal's notion that he is special, unique, and privileged. Sentimentality is challenged by forcing the offender to look at the pain he has inflicted on others and to dispense with the idea of doing good deeds when committing crimes. Super optimism is attacked by pointing out the destructiveness it carries for the offender. Underlying all of this is the ultimate choice the criminal must make: to die, to remain criminal and suffer the consequences, or to change to more responsible thinking and gain the rewards of a responsible lifestyle. If the client cannot be motivated by the awareness of these alternatives, then no counseling is possible.

Many techniques of cognitive/behavioral therapy can be used with criminal offenders and substance abusers alike (Beck et al. 1993; Samenow and Yochelson 1976; Stewart 1992; Ellis et al. 1988). Samenow (1984) provided several common sense suggestions for all counselors or therapists doing this work:

1.  Do not try to gain the client's approval. The client is not concerned with gaining the counselor's approval and will be manipulative of counselors who appear to need approval.

2.  Do not manipulate. This sets a bad example for the client.

3.  Avoid being either gullible or cynical.

4.  Be alert to the client's semantics. Words mean different things to criminals than to most people. For example, the word "respect" to the criminal means not to get in the way.

5.  Be prepared to terminate treatment if the client chooses not to cooperate. Remember that clients must make a basic choice about which direction they will take.

6.  Be direct without being provocative. It is important to be clear, but there is no need to engage the client in a power struggle.

7.  Be prepared to repeat things.

8.  Avoid playing detective.

9.  Control the interview politely.

Korn and McKorkle (1959) provided an interesting description of the accessibility of offender populations to intervention and change, which seemed to anticipate Prochaska's description of the stages of change (Prochaska and DiClemente 1992). The authors stated that most clients in institutions begin with a covert struggle for control. These clients have not recognized a need for change (precontemplators) and are likely to externalize blame for their problems. Counseling has little effect with such clients, but program staff should block the client's attempts to control.

At the next stage, the client begins to overtly rebel. The client is still unlikely to receive empathic interventions by program staff and treatment personnel. Staff should continue to apply clear and predictable consequences for misconduct.

Following this stage, the client begins heroic suffering by trying to gain sympathy for his plight from other clients in the program. He still accepts little personal responsibility, and most efforts to talk rationally with him fall on deaf ears.

After this, the client begins to feel despair. Many therapists respond, incorrectly, by attempting to shore up the client's self-esteem. Following Yochelson and Samenow's advice, the better approach would be to help clients see the full impact of their behavior on themselves and others. This would help clients to make a decision about the need for change. Clients in this stage may vacillate between taking personal responsibility and blaming others. Following the advice of Beutler and Consoli (1992), it is wise to assist the client in maintaining behavioral self-control rather than encouraging the client to ventilate his feelings.

Following the stage of despair is the stage of the emergence of self-doubt. At this point, the client finally begins to be open to intervention. In Prochaska's model, the client is beginning to contemplate the need for change and is beginning to internalize responsibility. Therapists should be careful about giving suggestions for specific change too quickly but should allow time for the client to fully realize his responsibility for his plight. Cognitive therapy tools are useful to help the client understand his thinking and see how it relates to behavior.

After this occurs, the next stage is one of behavior trials. In Prochaska's model, the client is in the preparation and action stages. Here, specific behavioral techniques can be used to help the client make changes.

The final stage, fixing therapeutic results, corresponds to Prochaska's maintenance stage. The client consolidates attitudinal, cognitive, and behavioral changes into new patterns. He internalizes changes and becomes self-reinforcing. The client recognizes errors in thinking and applies correctives independently.

This model stands in contrast to treatment models preferred for psychiatric populations, especially those with psychotic diagnoses (Korn and McCorkle 1959). Takahashi (1985) called for a supportive environment that communicates a sense of safety for the newly institutionalized patient. The patient progresses to a neutral stage in which the staff try to provide objective feedback to help patients learn about themselves. In the final stage, the treatment staff become more realistic. They offer their own thoughts and feelings and respond to the patient as one adult to another. By contrast, the antisocial client may try to take advantage of and manipulate an initially supportive environment and would not progress to the more neutral and realistic stages of treatment.

It is difficult to provide treatment for traditional psychiatric patients (those with schizophrenia and depression) on the same unit as patients with antisocial behavior (Johansen 1983; Gordon and Beresin 1983. See Goffman 1961 for a classic discussion of institutions). The antisocial clients are disruptive, and the treatment models for the two populations are different. It is difficult for staff to be supportive of one client but limit-setting for another client who breaks institutional rules without being attacked by the antisocial client for being unfair.

Most antisocial clients attempt to "split" the staff by complaining to one worker about another or trying to win sympathy from a particularly supportive worker to gain special treatment. Most correctional institutions end up with shifts pitted against one another as inmates complain to the A shift that the B shift lets them make extra phone calls, have extra juice, or have other privileges. Whether this is true or not, the A shift grows resentful of the B shift for letting the inmates get by with things, and soon the staff are fighting among themselves rather than running the institution.

Treatment and custodial staff often become alienated, especially if treatment staff take a lenient stance toward the inmate while custodial staff are required to set limits. These roles mirror the often-found polarization between the "task master" father figure and the warm and nurturing mother figure in the family (see Appendix E). Family therapy models (Bowen 1978; Riche 1979; Russell 1976) can work in institutional settings; the models also help illustrate how splitting can occur. When staff in programs disagree about a client and become polarized over the disagreement, they are divided (split) much as parents are when one wants to punish a child and the other wants to forgive. It is essential for effective treatment that all staff have a unified vision of treatment and effective communication about the activity of inmates or residents who are attempting to defeat the system by splitting it. If staff are working with different treatment theories, they interpret behavior differently and allow clients to drive a wedge between them (see Bayse [1995], *Working in Jails and Prisons: Becoming Part of the Team*, for a discussion of how offenders attempt to use one staff member against another).

Working with antisocial clients, especially in institutions, often boils down to managing day-to-day life and controlling rather than truly changing the client. Sometimes, however, these "hard core" clients do decide to change. It is difficult to know just what happens that causes someone to decide to change after years of irresponsibility. Some programs that are invulnerable to pressures from antisocial clients create a therapeutic environment where the client is forced into self-scrutiny.

Perhaps some people finally get sick and tired of being sick and tired. Some clients physically age or burn out on antisocial conduct. For other clients, confinement itself can help encourage the client's accessibility to intervention and provide motivation to change. Whatever the reason and however rarely it may happen, when a lifestyle offender decides to change, a good counselor can be very helpful, and the work is worthwhile.

# Chapter 8

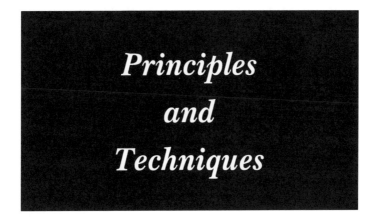

*Principles and Techniques*

*C*ounselors can learn techniques to overcome problems posed by difficult clients. Of course, specific skills are important in performing therapy, but as discussed earlier, specific techniques are not as important to the outcome of therapy as common factors, especially relationship factors, that cross theoretical boundaries. Nevertheless, some principles and skills may be useful.

Readers also should recognize that using an eclectic grab bag of techniques may result in a hodge podge approach to therapy with little focus or direction. So, readers should proceed with caution. However, most therapists probably have at least some conceptualization of their cases and the best treatment methods (Harris 1991).

## Set Expectations and Provide Structure

Two general principles of good therapy are to set expectations and to provide structure. Clients intent on subverting the counseling process can do so regardless of how explicit the counselor has been about such matters as appointment time, conduct in sessions, fees, objectives of sessions, and so on; thus, it is hopeless to try to clarify all the ground rules, especially in the initial session (Strean 1985).

Nevertheless, some rule setting may provide a basis for making clear decisions (Goodyear and Bradley 1980). As previously discussed, contracts between counselor and client are useful, but only when the client has truly participated in writing the agreement. Enright and Estep (1973) structured counseling by requiring clients who were ordered to complete a set number of sessions to meter their time. When not working productively, the meter was not allowed to run, thus extending the client's stay in therapy.

Other authors (Beck et al. 1993) recommend that every session should have a set agenda and that the therapist should provide a bridge between the present and the last session. Such structure may be too rigid for some therapists, but with managed care and limits on the number of therapy sessions, it is probably wise not to let therapy wander too much. On the other hand, many therapists find that a loose structure allows clients to gravitate toward issues they really need to discuss and that too tight a structure is inhibiting. The counselor should consider this issue and make a decision on it based on the client and the counselor's style.

## Maximize Choice, Minimize Demand

The principle of maximizing choice and minimizing demand also is helpful in working with treatment-resistant clients. When clients are reactive to coercion, they resent having their choices limited. Therefore, it may be helpful to try to give clients as many choices as possible about appointment times, topics to cover in sessions, and fee arrangements. Wherever possible, it is useful for the counselor to communicate the idea that the client has choices (although a choice between two negative options will hardly seem to be a choice to the client).

Seldom is it a good idea in the first session to spell out for the client all the changes that need to be made. Such laundry lists are discouraging to most treatment-resistant clients. They see only the mountains of work ahead and not the benefits. Solution-oriented approaches often avoid this problem by looking forward rather than backward. Homework assignments should be simple and manageable. When homework assignments are reviewed, the counselors should take care not to chastise clients for failure to work, though it is often helpful to explore the resistances behind clients not completing assignments.

## Allow Clients to Save Face

Another general principle for working with treatment-resistant clients is to help them save face whenever possible. Nobody likes to be brow–beaten. Selekman (1993) discussed how drug-using adolescents are very resistant to being labeled addicts or alcoholics, and this is true for most adults, as well. Avoiding pejorative labels is helpful in discussing the process of counseling. Instead of referring to the sessions as psychotherapy, it may be beneficial to call the work counseling or discussions. The less threatening the label the better. Cognitive therapists might want to refer to clients' irrational beliefs as "controversial" or "unhelpful," rather than "dysfunctional."

## Stimulate Clients to Think

Stimulating clients to think is a broad directive. To accomplish this, therapists may employ techniques that come from many approaches, including family therapy and cognitive behavioral theory. Cognitive therapy generally emphasizes collaboration between client and counselor to approach problems rationally and empirically. Thus, any strategy that helps clients think about themselves and their problem is useful. For example, cognitive therapists (Beck et al. 1993) discussed the uses of Socratic questioning (guided discovery) to help the client shift from externalizing blame to internalizing responsibility. Korn and McKorkle (1959) referred to this technique as detached questioning, the essence of which is to gently ask the client about his role in his predicament and his capacity to independently change what led to the problems.

Cognitive therapists frequently stimulate thinking by use of the advantages/disadvantages technique, which asks the client to list the pluses and minuses of a course of action. Cognitive therapists frequently challenge clients to discuss the evidence for or against a belief. These techniques are useful in creating reflection rather than reaction.

Many techniques from family and strategic therapies also stimulate clients to think. For example, scaling techniques ask clients to rate experiences on a continuum of one-to-ten or one-to-100. An adolescent might be asked, for instance, to rate how irritating his parents are on a ten-point scale. By doing so, the therapist interrupts either-or thinking and forces the client into some consideration of complexity. Questions asking clients to identify sequences of events help them to explore and challenge assumptions about linkages.

Circular questions about relationships force thoughtfulness about those relationships. For example, a reluctant probationer might be asked questions such as, "Who would be most likely to be upset if you terminated therapy and violated the terms of your probation?" or "Who would you least like to disappoint in your family by not completing your program?"

## Ignore Resistance

Many things are said or done in counseling that would have been better left untouched. For example, if a client in an institutional setting inappropriately attempts to form a special alliance with a counselor by gossiping about another staff member, the best tactic initially may be to change the subject rather than deal directly with the gossip—as long as the remark is mild and unlikely to cause any material consequences. Ignoring the client in this instance may allow time to establish a better relationship that would withstand the tension of a more direct discussion of the inappropriateness of a similar remark later. Timing is critical. It also may be appropriate to suggest that the client talk directly with the staff member. If the counselor offers to set up a three-way meeting to explore the complaint, most clients will quickly decline and stop complaining.

The counselor may often ignore angry or blaming remarks from clients. Counselors will have different beliefs and approaches to this. Some will prefer to deal with such problems as they arise. Particularly at the beginning of counseling, direct discussion of how the client is externalizing blame may result in the client feeling blamed. Some clients may test their counselors by telling fabricated, exaggerated stories to get shock reactions and to determine whether the counselor will maintain confidentiality. If the story becomes known to other staff members, the client knows who related it.

Regardless of the client's reason, even if it is to see whether the counselor is judgmental or trustworthy, counselors should take everything lightly and withhold reactions until they know more. This is a prudent strategy for avoiding premature termination of counseling because it allows clients to test the waters to see whether they want to come in. Counselors who work as part of a therapeutic team have the ethical obligation to let clients know with whom their case will be regularly discussed.

## Create Optimum Anxiety to Stimulate Self-Examination

Counselors are trained to work with people who become aware of a problem or get an uncomfortable feeling and ask for therapeutic help. These clients recognize the need for change because they want to feel better or because they realize their situation or problem, if left unchanged, will bring about undesirable consequences. Although they sense something is amiss, they may blame someone else for their unhappiness, anger, or anxiety, or they may view their unwanted situation as caused by factors outside their control. Nevertheless, they seek counseling because they hope to find a way to resolve the issue or because their anger seems unproductive and draining.

The involuntary client, on the other hand, often does not have anxiety or lacks awareness of it. Anger may exist, but the clients do not see this as inappropriate because they believe others are at fault. Most important, the righteousness of the anger prevents the client from considering how self-defeating his anger is. Thus, there is no motivation to change it.

If clients who are referred involuntarily to counseling do not express their feelings or avidly enlist the counselor to help them change a bad situation, how then should the counselor proceed? One possibility is to try to create anxiety or self-doubt in the person. A way of doing this is to point out inconsistencies between behavior and professed beliefs, or to point out how the person's choice of actions resulted in his present situation. Another method is to provide feedback about how others view and evaluate the person. The stronger the relationship between the counselor and the client, the more likely such methods will be tolerated by and beneficial to the client.

However, many clients will reject these attempts as unwelcome criticisms. This will be so, particularly for people who do not develop trust easily. Clients who do not have or are unaware of the usual anxiety will also deflect these techniques. A particular danger in confronting clients before a relationship is formed is that the counselor then becomes the adversary. Clients who are treatment resistant do not give counseling the benefit of a few warm-up sessions, which makes it difficult to time the confrontations appropriately. There is no opportunity for a client/counselor bond to form because the client does not let that happen. The trick is to create the anxiety without being blamed by the client for doing so. Much of the success that comes from doing this depends on style. Some counselors can smile while confronting their clients and the client does not link the negative confrontation with the "friendly" counselor. Nothing sticks to the "teflon" counselor.

While creating anxiety is often necessary, it also is true that much resistance stems from too much anxiety. Reducing anxiety, then, helps clients relax and take a more measured view of their situation (Young 1992). One technique for reducing anxiety is to "normalize" the problem. That is, the counselor should point out how many people are in a similar situation and how it is not a great personal aberration. For example, a man may be forced into treatment by his wife, who is upset at the provocative behavior between the father and daughter. The counselor may carefully point out that many men find themselves interested in their daughter's sexual development, but there is a line between appropriate and inappropriate interest that is sometimes crossed. By saying this, the counselor empathizes with the man's criticized feelings while clearly stating that acting on those feelings in sexual ways is inappropriate. The father may be relieved because he may have felt freakish and embarrassed at having feelings he could not prevent. This reduction of anxiety then frees him to explore acceptable ways of channeling his feelings.

Still another way of reducing anxiety is to ask questions in early sessions that do not tap material that is too sensitive. Sometimes taking a family history can be informative as it places the client in his or her social context. Asking a client to describe the personalities of different family members and the client's relationship with them can be revealing, and it is something most people can do without much prompting.

A technique related to creating anxiety is inducing frustration. Erickson (1980) described this technique as prompting a low-intensity response, then inhibiting it before it could be expressed. For example, in a family meeting, a reticent child might be asked a question then denied the opportunity to answer by a quick change of subject. The frustration in the child builds until he is bursting with something to say.

Gestalt therapists create a similar effect by trying to create awareness in the client without giving any indication of how that awareness should be channeled. A counselor might point out how the client is clenching his teeth, but the counselor does not then interpret what the clenching means. The induced awareness of the behavior brings into consciousness the client's unfinished business, which is frustrating, and the client then becomes motivated to resolve what is incomplete. The counselor, who refuses to take responsibility for what the behavior means, forces the client to do so. Thus, Erickson creates tension by frustrating a response. Gestalt therapists similarly create tension by inducing awareness of unfinished business (Young 1992).

## Time Interventions for Critical Moments

Another tactic is not to try to create anxiety or discomfort, but to wait until clients are suffering as a natural consequence of their actions, such as catching alcoholics when their world is crumbling around them or criminals when the awesome reality of imprisonment seems imminent. Timing interventions this way tends to keep the counselor out of the adversary role. Unfortunately, however, many counselors want to ease their clients' pain at these moments by offering reassurance or by enhancing their self-esteem. Instead, what is often necessary is a persistent, but not cruel, inventory of the person and assessment of the situation (Samenow 1984).

Counselors have to learn to do concentrated work while the client is open to it. Weekly sessions may fail because the client's defenses will be reconstructed between sessions. Counselors should not be too harsh on their clients while they are depressed or unhappy, but they should not do their clients' work for them, either. The difficulty with this approach is that it is not preventive, and the client's life is already chaotic before openness to counseling occurs. By then, the crisis tends to turn counseling either into emotional exchanges or to strategizing about how to escape the immediate crisis, rather than attempting to mutually determine the roots of the problem and encouraging the client to accept personal responsibility for it.

## Pique Curiosity

A difficult method of engaging reluctant clients is to intrigue them and pique their curiosity. Yochelson and Samenow (1976, 1977) described how they give clients a lengthy description of their hunches about their behavior and thoughts about work, school, friendships, and family. The accuracy of the unflattering portrait disarms criminals who wonder how someone who does not know them knows them so well.

A variation is to make a prediction about the client's behavior. For example, batterers whose wives have left them are usually distraught and seek counseling because their wives demand it before they will consider reconciliation. Counselors can point out that the man's motivation to continue counseling will dissipate as soon as his wife returns.

Some men are quite aware of their intent but are intrigued with the counselor's insight and conduct (assuming that the counselor has declined requests to strategize about how to get the woman to return rather than how to change the violent behavior). Other men may deny to themselves that they lack a sincere interest in counseling except as a device to get their wives back, but the truth will become clear over time, and the accuracy of the earlier assessment can be pointed out later to weaken the man's self-assured certainty.

Sometimes psychological tests make clients curious and willing to talk, if for no other reason than to satisfy a curiosity about themselves, much like the desire to see pictures of oneself in various poses or costumes. Some clients, however, treat testing as an opportunity to manipulate or make fun of the counselor, and then, the testing results must be treated with caution.

## Identify Positive Intent

People who are involuntarily referred to counseling are usually in conflict with other people, either legally or socially. When such a conflict exists, parties to the conflict tend to view each other's motivations negatively. Parents who are having trouble with a rebellious child frequently say the child is being stubborn or selfish. However, it is possible for the counselor to put the child's behavior in a different light and soften hostility by saying he is showing signs of wanting to be independent, a praise-worthy characteristic of anyone soon to become an adult. Many behaviors that are ordinarily viewed negatively are perhaps done for basically positive and human reasons. If the underlying motivation can be understood, the counselor is in a better position to be empathic and nonjudgmental toward the client, and so the counseling process will be aided. Anderson and Stewart (1983), Teismann (1980), and Watzlawick et al. (1967, 1974) offer extended discussions of relabeling, reframing, and positive intent.

Identifying positive intent in the involuntary client is a precondition for use of many powerful paradoxical techniques. Tennen et al. (1981) described defiance-based paradoxical prescriptions as successful because the client rebels against the counselor's interpretation of a positively motivated negative behavior. For example, a client who does not say much in therapy might be praised and encouraged to continue to be very thoughtful about what he says. A client who is argumentative in a family meeting might be praised for being so involved and active.

Often, the counselor has no actual power to stop a client's behavior. However, if the counselor defines the behavior as positive and insists that it is what he or she wants, the client may stop it. For example, the counselor may be annoyed that during a group counseling session, two group members talk to each other and exclude the other members. So, the two may be gently teased and encouraged to provide barely audible background noise so that the rest of the group can continue. The counselor then provides feedback on their noise level and lets them know if they are too soft or too loud. By "taking control" this way, the counselor has prevented the clients from excluding and disrupting the other group members. The counselor may not be able to directly control a behavior but can indirectly do so by changing some part of it.

As implied earlier, perhaps the most important benefit from looking for positive intent in an otherwise negative behavior comes from the increased empathy the counselor can feel toward the client. Clients who appear rebellious, uncooperative, angry, and uncommunicative can be viewed positively as wanting self-determination (Riordan et al. 1978). Counselors who recognize this motivation are less likely to be critical or to try to impose unnecessary restrictions on the client that would increase rebellious behavior and undermine the development of a therapeutic alliance.

Empathy and acceptance of the client are, in fact, the ultimate paradox of counseling. When the counselor understands and acknowledges the reluctance that clients have about changing, clients feel free to change. For example, when the counselor understands that the alcoholic has not quit drinking because of the risk of losing drinking buddies, the client becomes freer to consider quitting as an option. The more the counselor emphasizes the reason for changing, the more the client reacts with the reasons why change is not possible. The more the counselor empathizes with the risks of changing, the greater the client's freedom is to consider the advantages of changing.

While it is important to try to look for the positive intent behind negative behaviors, counselors need to consider that such intent may not always be present. Yochelson and Samenow (1976, 1977), for example, viewed the motivations of the offender as egocentric and irresponsible. They described the criminal as being interested in the excitement of criminal activity rather than in the dull pleasure of a responsible life. They stated that criminals view themselves as unique people who should not be subjected to the rules that govern ordinary people. The criminal was further described as one who wants power over others for personal benefit.

Juveniles who are truant from school may be unconsciously reacting to stress by trying to attract their parents' attention to keep them from arguing between themselves; children suffer less stress from being truant than from worrying about their parents' arguments. On the other hand, some criminal children may be truant because they are simply bored with the demands of school and prefer the excitement of street life. To be successful at finding positive intent, counselors need to have an understanding of their clients' underlying personality structures and interpersonal interactions. This boils down to understanding what end is served by apparently illogical, self-damaging behavior.

Naive paradoxical prescriptions also should be avoided. For example, suicidal patients should not be instructed to "go ahead and do it." These simplistic prescriptions are not paradoxical at all; they are dangerous.

## Use Nonverbal Techniques

Perhaps the most simple thing to try when dealing with a client who is reluctant to talk is to "talk about not talking" by exploring the reasons for staying silent. Sometimes clients have difficulty using language to describe their experiences. A method to use when working with difficult nonverbal clients is to engage them in physical activities, such as crafts, sports, or survival-skill expeditions.

People of all ages and types can learn much about themselves through involvement in survival tests. Situations that expose clients to new stimuli also may have educational value. They are especially useful because clients get caught up in the experience and find themselves participating to survive, emotionally and physically. Encounter groups using the "hot-seat" have a similar quality. Rooney (1992) described work with involuntary clients in groups and families, noting the power of peers to be both positive and negative role models. Much of this social learning is nonverbal and difficult to replicate in individual therapy where the therapist is not necessarily a role model for the client. Learning in groups is often achieved because peers can accept confrontation better from each other than from an authority figure such as a therapist.

**Capitalize on Various Styles of Learning and Change**. Unfortunately, counselors often assume that the client is resistant rather than consider the possibility that they have used an inadequate approach (Lazarus and Fay 1983). It is too simplistic to always attribute lack of progress in counseling to the client's resistance.

Involuntary clients are not as likely as voluntary clients to adapt to the counselor's style. That is, an involuntary client who agrees to participate after some preliminary talking may not remain convinced that counseling is valuable if the counselor's approach does not seem sensible as the sessions progress.

Imagine that a wife talks her husband into trying counseling. The man has a high school diploma and operates heavy machinery for a living. The counselor begins by taking an extensive family history, including information about the couple's parents and grandparents. The wife enjoys this discussion, but the husband does not because he does not see how it relates to their problems. Regardless of how theoretically relevant the information is, a present-focused, action-oriented man who was reluctant to enter counseling in the first place will soon renew his reluctance and resist coming to counseling. It is important, then, to try to adapt to clients rather than stick religiously to an approach that might drive them away.

People learn in different ways. It is especially important to consider the learning style of the involuntary client. A brief listing of ways that people change should highlight some approaches that counselors may consider.

1. **Insight**. Gaining insight into your own thoughts and behavior is the basis for much counseling, but many people do not change behavior through better cognitive understanding, or they find that understanding hard to achieve. Other methods may be necessary to communicate a message.

2. **Modeling**. Some clients will learn best by seeing the appropriate behavior displayed. Counselors can demonstrate the behavior themselves or arrange a demonstration.

3. **Behavior rehearsal.** This is the "try it, you'll like it" technique. Clients may grudgingly agree to try on a new behavior, then discover they like it. Role-playing often follows demonstration demonstration of the behavior and is followed by a real trial of the behavior. For example, a client who needs to learn how to express feeling may observe a counselor's self-disclosure, then practice self-disclosure in role-playing with the counselor before trying to talk openly with friends or family members.

4. **Self-esteem.** Some people improve in all areas of functioning when they feel better about themselves. This enhancement of self-image is most often made possible by achievement and recognition, not direct discussion of self-worth.

5. **Relationships.** Some people improve in the presence of an empathic counselor or friend who allows them to open up and be themselves without criticism or judgment.

6. **Group pressure.** The power of the emotional field of the group and family is strong. Peer cultures may work better than individual therapy. Sometimes it is easier to help the client change by influencing the family first. Sometimes the client may not be able to respond to direct suggestions whereas family members can. Thus, the path of least resistance (and effort) may be through a slightly circuitous route.

7. **Reinforcement.** Much behavior is influenced by reaction to it in the environment. An unresponsive environment inadequately rewards behavior change. It is often difficult for counselors to affect the external environment, but sometimes this is possible. For example, a child having difficulty in school may be helped by having the teacher or principal arrange immediate feedback and praise for slight improvements in the child's behavior that previously may have been overlooked.

# Chapter 9

## Conclusions and Recommendations

## Suggestions for Effective Psychotherapy and Overcoming Treatment Resistance

1. Empathize with the client's anger and resentment at being coerced into treatment. Work to create hope. Disassociate from the coercion. Help the client to see the benefits of being in treatment. It is not possible to work on the problem that prompted the referral until the client overcomes his resistance to being in therapy.

2. Give people a little time to tell their story and feel that their problems are understood. Developing a therapeutic alliance is essential to successful therapy with most clients. Even in brief-therapy models there must be some effort to see clients' problems through their eyes.

3. Try to find out what made the person come in for therapy: What is the problem, and why did it bring the client in now rather than at some other time? It is important to learn what the client's theory is about the nature and seriousness of the problem.

4. Whose idea was it to seek therapy? If your client is present at the request of someone else, clarify the goals. The desire for change and the responsibility for change generally need to exist in the same person. Find out what behaviors the client is motivated to change.

5. Unless you are an analyst who attempts to be impersonal, communicate the idea that you like your clients and are interested in them, but do not gush. Be clear about the boundaries in the relationship. The counselor needs to know and communicate the difference between friendship and a caring professional relationship.

6. Clients usually expect therapy to be shorter than therapists expect. Experienced therapists may see many behavior patterns that need changing, but most clients do not want a complete overhaul and may not even see a need for a tune-up. Let the customer decide what services are needed. Clients who are reluctant to be in therapy need to receive some help to see the benefits of treatment.

7. Confront at your own peril. Learn to say things in a way that clients can hear without feeling threatened. This applies doubly for reactive clients. The fact that there is limited time to do therapy does not mean that the use of confrontation will speed up the process. It is more likely to derail it.

8. When they seek counseling and at various stages of counseling, some clients are not aware that they need to change anything, or if they think there is a problem, they blame someone else for it. Some know they need to change but do not know what change is needed. Others know

what to change but do not know how. The type of work that you do will change, accordingly. Improve your techniques for raising the consciousness of the client to help him prepare better for behavior change.

9. Give consideration to the appropriate setting, format, and frequency of treatment. Some people need groups. Some need individual help. Some clients need to meet daily, others weekly or monthly. Clients are affected by the reception they get in the therapist's office from support personnel. It is important that the staff act in a professional way and that the office conveys a professional image.

10. Coach clients on how to be good clients. Let them know what they need to do to be helped. Active clients are successful clients. Most people are unfamiliar with therapy and need to be educated about how it works. Give homework assignments but anticipate that many clients do not have the discipline to follow through with difficult assignments.

11. If your approach is not working, try something else. Therapy is still a subjective art. Clinicians need to be flexible in therapy and recognize that there is no one right way to do therapy with all clients.

12. If your client is too similar to you, what do you have to teach? It is important to consider your client's level of development and to ask whether you are prepared to be a model for your client. It is not necessary to be perfect to be a good counselor, but it is helpful not to be currently struggling with the same problem the client is. Counselors who are recovering alcoholics are not likely to help a practicing alcoholic if the counselors cannot remain sober themselves. Counselors who are not a step ahead of the client should probably make a referral.

13. If your client is too dissimilar to you, will what you have to teach be relevant? It is easy to misjudge clients who come from different racial and socioeconomic backgrounds. This is a special problem with coerced clients, who are disproportionately from minority groups. Counselors cannot change their race or sex, but they can work to develop cultural sensitivity to understand the viewpoint of the clients they are counseling.

14. Do not forget the value of psychiatric medication. Also, remember that people have bodies that can be sick, and this may play a role in their behavior. Clients with depressive and psychotic illnesses often benefit from medication. The field of biological psychiatry is making amazing advances that should not be ignored. Getting a medical consultation is good practice.

15. Slower is often faster. It is important not to rush therapy even if managed care limits the number of sessions. Clients often do not reveal the real reason they came to therapy until they have decided that they can trust the therapist. Coerced clients are especially slow to trust the therapist with any important information.

16. Many treatment-resistant clients are men. Understanding the special binds that men feel in this culture is essential to working with men who reject psychotherapy and believe it to be of no value to them.

17. Cynicism is a special roadblock to forming a therapeutic alliance. Cynicism reflects a basic mistrust of people and of the potential for solving problems through interpersonal relationships. Recognizing the signs of cynicism and learning to respond to them will improve the development of a therapeutic relationship.

18. The demands of managed care cannot dictate how therapy is done. It is fine to look for more efficient ways to do therapy and to select treatment goals that are consistent

with the funding available. It is not reasonable to attempt major personality changes in ten sessions.

19. Counselors should be realistic about setting treatment goals with antisocial clients and should be careful not to attempt relationship therapies without great care.

20. Client confidentiality is no less important because the client has been coerced into treatment. Respect for the client's right to ultimately refuse treatment is essential.

*Bibliography*

American Psychiatric Association. 1987. *Diagnostic and statistical manual.* Vol. III (Revised). Washington, D.C.

———. 1994. *Diagnostic and statistical manual.* Vol IV. Washington, D.C.

American Psychological Association. 1978. Report of the task force on the role of psychology in the criminal justice system. *American Psychologist* 33 (12): 160-65.

———. 1993. Division 41. Committee on ethical guidelines for forensic psychology. Washington, D.C.

Anderson, C., and S. Stewart. 1983. *Mastering resistance.* New York: Guilford Press.

Ansbacher, H. L. 1981. Prescott Lecky's concept of resistance and his personality. *Journal of Clinical Psychology* 37: 791-95.

Arcaya, J. 1978. Coercive counseling and self-disclosure. *International Journal of Offender Therapy* 22 (3): 231-37.

Basch, M. 1982. Dynamic psychotherapy and its frustrations. In *Resistance: psychodynamic and behavioral approaches*. Edited by P. Wachtel. New York: Plenum Press.

Bayse, D. J. 1995. *Working in jails and prisons: Becoming part of the team*. Laurel, Md.: American Correctional Association.

Beck, A.; F. Wright; C. Newman; and B. Liese. 1993. *Cognitive therapy of substance abuse*. New York: Guilford Press.

Benson, M. 1985. Denying the guilty mind: Accounting for involvement in a white collar crime. *Criminology* 23 (4): 583-608.

Berman, E., and R. Segel. 1982. The captive client: Dilemmas of psychotherapy in the psychiatric hospital. *Psychotherapy: Theory, Research, and Practice.* 19: 31-42.

Bernbaum, M. 1960. Right to treatment. *American Bar Association Journal* 56: 499.

Berne, E. 1964. *Games people play*. New York: Grove Press.

Biracree, T., and N. Biracree. 1988. *Almanac of the American people*. New York: Facts on File.

Blanchard, G. 1995. *The difficult connection: The therapeutic relationship in sex offender treatment*. Brandon, Vermont: Safer Society Press.

Bowen, M. 1978. *Family therapy in clinical practice*. New York: Jason Aronson.

Bratter, T. 1974. Helping those who do not want to help themselves: A reality and confrontation orientation. *Corrective and Social Psychiatry and Journal of Behavior Technology, Methods and Therapy* 20 (4): 23-30.

Brehm, J. W. 1966. *A theory of psychological reactance*. New York: Academic Press.

Brownell, A. 1981. Counseling men through bodywork. *Personnel and Guidance Journal* 60 (4): 252-55.

Buetler, L., and A. Consoli. 1992. Systematic eclectic psychotherapy. In *Handbook of psychotherapy integration*. Edited by J. C. Norcross and M. R. Goldfried. New York: Basic Books.

Charny, I. 1982. How can we commit the unthinkable? *Genocide: the human cancer*. Boulder, Colorado: Westview Press.

Collins, A. 1969. *The lonely and afraid: Counseling the hard to reach*. New York: Odyssey Press.

Corey, G.; M. Corey; P. Callahan; and J. Russell. 1982. *Group techniques*. Belmont, California: Wadsworth, Inc.

Cressey, D. *Other people's money: A study in the social psychology of embezzlement*. Glencoe, Ill.: Free Press.

Diuguid, L. 1995. Treatment in need of treatment. *K.C. Star*, 4 March.

Dowd, D., and F. Wallbrown. 1993. Motivational components of client reactance. *Journal of Counseling and Development* 71: 533-37.

Duehn, W. D., E. K. Proctor. 1977. Initial client interaction and premature discontinuance in treatment. *American Journal of Orthopsychiatry* 47: 284-90.

Dyer, W., and J. Vriend. 1973. Counseling the reluctant client. *Journal of Counseling Psychology* 20: 240-46.

Elkin, M. 1984. *Families under the influence*. New York: W.W. Norton.

Ellis, A. 1985. *Overcoming resistance*. New York: Springer Publishing Company.

Ellis, A.; J. McInerney; R. DiGiuseppe; and R. Yeager. 1988. *Rational-emotive therapy with alcoholics and substance abusers*. New York: Pergamon Press.

Enright, J., and R. Estep. 1973. Metered counseling for the reluctant client. *Psychotherapy: Theory, Research, and Practice* 10: 305-7.

Epperson, D. L.; D. J. Bushway; and R. E. Warman. 1983. Client self-terminations after one counseling session: Effects of problem recognition, counselor gender, and counselor experience. *Journal of Counseling Psychology* 30: 307-15.

Erickson, M. 1980. Resistant patient. In *The nature of hypnosis and suggestion*. Vol. 1. Edited by E. L. Rosse. New York: Irvington Publishers, 229-30.

Farrell, W. 1993. *The myth of male power*. New York: Simon and Schuster.

Forest, G. 1982. *Confrontation in psychotherapy of the alcoholic*. Holmes Beach, Fla.: Learning Publications, Inc.

Fox, V. 1985. *Introduction to corrections*. Englewood Cliffs, N.J.: Prentice-Hall.

Friedman, L. 1993. *Crime and punishment in American history*. New York: Basic Books.

Frankl, V. 1960. Paradoxical intention: A logotherapeutic technique. *American Journal of Psychotherapy*. 14: 520-35.

Garfield, S. 1992. Eclectic psychotherapy: A common factors approach. In *Handbook of psychotherapy integration*. Edited by J. C. Norcross and M. R. Goldfried. New York: Basic Books.

Geiser, M., and W. Annitto. 1985. Trafficking drug addicts: Some thoughts on the interchange between the criminal justice and mental health systems. Paper presented at Annual Meeting of the Academy of Criminal Justice Sciences.

Gitterman, A. 1983. Uses of resistance: A transactional view. *Social Work* 28 (2): 127-31.

Glasser, W. 1965. *Reality therapy.* New York: Harper and Row.

Goffman, E. 1961. *Asylums.* New York: Anchor Books.

Goodyear, R. K., and F. O. Bradley. 1980. The helping process as contractual. *Personnel and Guidance Journal* 58: 512-15.

Gordon, C., and E. Beresin. 1983. Conflicting treatment models for the inpatient management of borderline patients. *American Journal of Psychiatry* 140 (18): 979-83.

Green, G. 1990. *Occupational crime.* Chicago: Nelson-Hall.

Haley, J. 1963. *Strategies of psychotherapy.* New York: Grune and Stratton.

Haley, J. 1983. *Uncommon therapy: The psychiatric techniques of Milton Erickson.* New York: Norton.

Harris, G. 1984. An interview with Stanton Samenow, co-author of *The criminal personality. Journal of Counseling and Development* 63 (4): 227-29.

———. 1987. Influence of reasoning, disagreement and democratic decision making on levels of domestic violence. *Journal of Justice Issues* (2) 1: 33-41.

———. 1991(a). Eclecticism, again. *Journal of Mental Health Counseling* (13) 4: 427-31.

Harris, G., ed. 1991(b). *Tough customers: Counseling unwilling clients.* Laurel, Md.: American Correctional Association.

Harris, G., ed. 1991(c). Counseling the white collar offender. In *Tough customers: Counseling unwilling clients.* Laurel Md.: American Correctional Association.

Harris, G., and N. Kirk. 1983(a). A behavior continuum: A look at the personality disorders. *Journal of Offender Counseling* 6 (1): 2-8.

————. 1983(b). A behavior continuum: The need for an interdisciplinary approach. Paper presented at Annual Meeting of the Academy of Criminal Justice Sciences.

Harris, G., and D. Watkins. 1987. *Counseling the involuntary and resistant client.* College Park, Md.: American Correctional Association.

Hartman, H. 1979. Interviewing techniques in probation and parole. *Federal Probation.* 43: 55-62, 60-66.

Heitler, H. 1976. Preparatory techniques in initiating expressive psychotherapy with lower-class, unsophisticated patients. *Psychological Bulletin* 83: 339-52.

Heitler, S. 1990. *From conflict to resolution.* New York: W. W. Norton.

Ivey, A. 1983. *International Interviewing and Counseling.* Monterey, Calif.: Brooks/Cole.

Johansen, K. 1983. The impact of patients with chronic character pathology on a hospital inpatient unit. *Hospital and Community Psychiatry* 34 (9): 842-46.

Kanter, D., and P. Mirvis. 1989. *The cynical Americans.* San Francisco: Jossey-Bass.

Kittrie, N. 1971. *The right to be different: Deviance under forced therapy.* Baltimore: Johns Hopkins Press.

Kloss, J., and J. Karan. 1979. Community intervention for reluctant clients. *Federal Probation* 43: 37-43.

Korn, R., and L. McCorkle. 1959. *Criminology and penology.* New York: Rinehart and Winston.

Kramer, S. 1985. A systemwide approach to sex offender treatment and tracking. Paper presented at Annual Meeting of the Academy of Criminal Justice Sciences.

Lambert, M. 1992. Psychotherapy outcome research: Implications for integrative and eclectic therapists. In *Handbook of psychotherapy integration*. Edited by J. C. Norcross and M. R. Goldfried. New York: Basic Books.

Larke, J. 1985. Compulsory treatment: Some practical methods of treating the mandated client. *Psychotherapy* 22 (2): 262-68.

Larrabee, M. J. 1982. Working with reluctant clients through affirmation techniques. *Personnel and Guidance Journal* 61: 105-9.

Lasch, C. 1978. *The culture of narcissism: American life in an age of diminishing expectation*. New York: Norton.

Lawson, D. 1995. Conceptualization and treatment for Vietnam veterans experiencing posttraumatic stress disorder. *Journal of Mental Health Counseling* (17) 1: 31-53.

Lazarus, A. 1992. Multimodal therapy. In *Handbook of psychotherapy integration*. Edited by J. C. Norcross and M. R. Goldfried. New York: Basic Books.

Lazarus, A., and A. Fay. 1983. Resistance or rationalization. In *Resistance: Psychodynamic and behavior approaches*. Edited by P. Watchel. New York: Plenum Press, 115-32.

Lineham, M. 1993. *Cognitive-behavioral treatment of borderline personality disorder*. New York: Guilford Press.

Lion, J., and W. Reid, eds. 1985. *Assaults within psychiatric facilities*. Orlando: Harcourt Brace Jovanovich.

May, R. 1969. *Love and will*. New York: Dell Publishing.

McCarthy, B. R., and B. J. McCarthy. 1984. *Community-based corrections*. Monterey, Calif.: Brooks/Cole.

Meloy, R., A. Haroun, and E. Schiller. 1990. *Clinical guidelines for involuntary outpatient treatment*. Sarasota, Fla.: Professional Resource Exchange.

Menninger, K. 1958. *Theory of psychoanalytic technique*. New York: Harper and Row.

———. 1968. *The crime of punishment*. New York: The Viking Press.

Messer, S. 1992. A critical examination of belief structures in integrative and eclectic psychotherapy. In *Handbook of psychotherapy integration*. Edited by J. C. Norcross and M. R. Goldfried. New York: Basic Books.

Miller, W. 1985. Motivation for treatment: A review with special emphasis on alcoholism. *Psychological Bulletin* 98 (1): 84-107.

Millon, T. 1986. A theoretical derivation of pathological personalities. In *Contemporary directions in psychopathology: Toward the DSM-IV*. Edited by T. Millon and G.L. Klerman. New York: Guilford Press.

Millon, T., and C. L. Klerman, eds. 1986. *Contemporary directions in psychopathology: Toward the DSM-IV*. New York: Guilford Press.

Minor, W. 1981. Techniques of neutralization: a reconceptualization and empirical validation. *Journal of Research in Crime and Delinquency* 18: 295-318.

Monahan, J., ed. 1980. *Who is the client? The ethics of psychological intervention in the criminal justice system*. Washington, D.C.: American Psychological Association.

National Institute for Juvenile Justice and Delinquency Prevention. Office of Juvenile Justice and Delinquency Prevention. Law Enforcement Assistance Administration. U.S. Department of Justice.

1983. *Intervening with convicted serious juvenile offenders.* Washington, D.C.: U. S. Government Printing Office.

Norcross, J. C., and M. R. Goldfried, eds. 1992. *Handbook of psychotherapy integration.* New York: Basic Books.

Osherson, S. 1992. *Wrestling with love.* New York: Basic Books.

Otani, A. 1989. Client resistance in counseling: Its theoretical rationale and taxonomic classification. *Journal of Counseling and Development* 67 (8): 458-61.

Palmer, S. E. 1983. Authority: An essential part of social work practice. *Social Work Journal* 28 (2): 120-25.

Paradise, L., and D. Wilder. 1979. The relationship between client and counseling effectiveness. *Counselor Education and Supervision* 19: 35-41.

Patterson, C. 1980. *Theories of counseling and personality.* New York: Harper and Row.

Peck, M. S. 1983. *People of the lie.* New York: Simon and Schuster.

Pekarik, G. 1985. Coping with dropouts. *Professional Psychology* 16 (1): 114-123.

Pekarik, G.; D. Jones; and C. Blodgett. 1986. Personality and demographics characteristics of dropouts and completers in a nonhospital residential alcohol treatment program. *International Journal of the Addictions* 21: 131-37.

Prochaska, J., and C. DiClemente. 1992. The transtheoretical approach. In *Handbook of psychotherapy integration.* Edited by J. C. Norcross and M. R. Goldfried. New York: Basic Books.

Riche, M. 1979. Integrating families into a healing community: The use of structured and strategic family therapy in a psychodynamically oriented hospital. Unpublished paper, Menninger Foundation.

Rigazio-DiGilio, S., and I. Ivey. 1993. Systemic cognitive-developmental therapy: An integrative framework. *The Family Journal* 1 (3): 208-19.

Riordan, R. J.; K. B. Matheny; and C. Harris. 1978. Helping counselors minimize client reluctance. *Counselor Education and Supervision* 18 (1): 14-22.

Robison, F.; M. Smaby; and G. Donovan. 1989. Influencing reluctant elderly clients to participate in mental health counseling. *Journal of Mental Health Counseling* 11 (3): 259-72.

Rooney, R. 1992. *Strategies for work with involuntary clients.* New York: Columbia University Press.

Rupple, G., and T. Kaul. 1982. Investigation of social influence theory's conception of client resistance. *Journal of Counseling Psychology* 29: 305-7.

Russel, A. 1976. Limitations of family therapy. *Clinical Social Work Journal* 4: 83-92.

Samenow, S. 1984. *Inside the criminal mind.* New York: Times Books.

Selekman, M. 1993. *Pathways to change: Brief therapy solutions with difficult adolescents.* New York: Guilford Press.

Shertzer, B., and S. Stone. 1974. *Fundamentals of counseling.* Boston: Houghton Mifflin.

Smith, A., and L. Berlin. 1988. *Treating the criminal offender.* 3d ed. New York: Plenum Press.

Solzhenitsyn, A. 1963. *One day in the life of Ivan Denisovich.* New York: Bantam Books.

Stewart, J. 1993. Rehabilitation counseling with the criminal offender in the community setting. *Directions in Rehabilitation Counseling* 3(5): 3-28.

Straus, M., and R. Gelles. 1986. Societal change and change in family violence from 1975 to 1985 as revealed by two national surveys. *Journal of Marriage and the Family* 48 (August): 465-79.

Strean, H. 1985. *Resolving resistances in psychotherapy.* New York: John Wiley.

Streib, V. 1988. *American executions of female offenders: A preliminary inventory of names, dates, and other information.* Cleveland, Ohio: Cleveland Marshall College of Law.

Sykes, G., and D. Matza. 1957. Techniques of neutralization: A theory of delinquency. *American Sociological Review* 22: 667-70.

Takahashi, T. 1985. Psychodynamic treatment in an in-patient hospital setting. Unpublished paper. Topeka, Kans.: Menninger Foundation.

Teismann, M. 1980. Convening strategies in family therapy. *Family Progress* 19: 373-400.

Tennen, H.; M. Rohrbaugh; S. Press; and L. White. 1981. Reactance theory and therapeutic paradox: A compliance/defiance model. *Psychotherapy: Theory, Research and Practice* 18 (1): 14-22.

Twohey, D., and M. Ewing. 1995. The male voice of emotional intimacy. *Journal of Mental Health Counseling* (17) 1: 54-62.

U.S. Bureau of Health and Human Services. 1993. National Center for Health Statistics. Monthly vital statistics report. Vol. 2, part A. Washington, D.C.: Health and Human Services.

Van Hoose, W. H., and J. A. Kottler. 1985. *Ethical issues in counseling and psychotherapy.* San Francisco: Jossey-Bass.

Varga, L. 1971. Motivational intervention: Theoretical considerations in employment counseling. *Journal of Employment Counseling* 8 (3): 137-44.

Vontress, C. 1974. Barriers in cross-cultural counseling. *Counseling and Values* 18 (3): 160-65.

Wachtel, P., ed. 1982. *Resistance: Psychodynamic and behavioral approaches.* New York: Plenum Press.

Walters, G. 1990. *The criminal lifestyle: Patterns of serious criminal conduct.* Newbury Park, Calif.: Sage Publications.

Ward, D. 1984. Termination of individual counseling. *Journal of Counseling and Development* 63 (1) :21-26.

Watzlawick, P.; J. Beavin; and D. Jackson. 1967. *Pragmatics of human communication.* New York: Norton.

Watzlawick, P.; J. H. Weakland; and R. Fisch. 1974. *Change: Principles of problem formation and problem resolution.* New York: Norton.

Weiss, J. 1993. *How psychotherapy works.* New York: Guildford Press.

Welo, B. 1995. *Life beyond loss: A workbook for incarcerated men.* Laurel, Md.: American Correctional Association.

West, M. 1975. Building a relationship with the unmotivated client. *Psychotherapy: Theory, Research and Practice* 12: 48-51.

Yochelson, S., and S. Samenow. 1976. *The criminal personality: Profile for change.* New York: Jason Aronson.

————. 1977. *The criminal personality: The change process.* New York: Jason Aronson.

Young, M. E. 1992. *Counseling methods and techniques--An eclectic approach.* New York: Merrill.

Young, J. 1990. *Cognitive therapy for personality disorders.* Sarasota, Fla.: Professional Resource Exchange.

## Introduction to Exercises

The following appendices provide counselors and counselors-in-training with an opportunity to update their skills. These exercises may be used as part of in-service training or in conjunction with a course in counseling or psychology.

# Appendix A

## Reasons for Resisting Treatment

1. List all the reasons why a client might resist entering treatment.

2. List general reasons why clients might resist changing once in treatment.

3. Finally, list general reasons why various clients might resist you as a therapist.

4. Think of a time when you resisted doing something that someone in authority wanted you to do. How did you react? What were your feelings?

5. Now, think of a time when someone had you do something that you did not want to do? How were you persuaded?

6. Think of a time when you persuaded someone (other than a client) to do something. What methods did you use? Did they work?

# Appendix B

## Force-Field Analysis

On either side of a line dividing a two-dimensional plane, imagine forces pushing the line to one direction or another. If all the forces are on one side of the line, the line moves easily, but if the forces are divided fairly evenly on both sides of the line, the line stays immobilized—the irresistible force meets the immovable object. When clients are "stuck," it is because there are equally strong forces for and against movement. It is often easy to see the very good reasons why a client "should" change, but not so easy to see why the client "should not" change. The counselor's tendency is to begin to point out to the client all the reasons to change, but this often has the paradoxical effect of creating strength in the forces opposed to change. Sometimes it is helpful to empathize supremely with the client's reasons for not changing. The task here is to create a force-field analysis that will visually display the forces on either side of the line for a given client.

It is especially helpful to draw these force-field analyses for the client's resistance to counseling, change, and the counselor. Breaking down resistance into these three parts helps identify it more specifically and improves treatment planning at various stages of the treatment process.

|  | Counseling | Change | Counselor |
|---|---|---|---|
| Why the client should change |  |  |  |
| Why the client should not change |  |  |  |

# Appendix C

## Responding to Ambivalence

On the force-field analysis you identified pressures that a client might feel about counseling, change, and the counselor. When counseling, we often fail to understand the client's ambivalence in the counseling relationship and how the client values change. A useful strategy is to empathize with the side of the ambivalence that is hidden. For example, some counselors might pressure an alcoholic into quitting drinking by giving all the logical reasons why this would be good to do. An alternative approach is to empathize with the reasons why quitting would be a problem. ("If you quit, where would you find friends with whom to socialize?" "If you quit, would you have to begin to deal with other problems in your relationship with your spouse?")

Most clients have been lectured repeatedly on why they ought to change. So, hearing someone empathize with their fear of change is a liberating experience and allows them to more fully consider their range of choices.

List the negative effects that you think the following changes might have on someone:

- stopping drinking

- quitting smoking

- returning to school

- getting into a committed relationship

# Appendix D

## Script for Involuntary Client Role Play

The client is a twenty-year-old male with a history of alcohol abuse. He has had one serious car accident under the influence of alcohol, for which his license was suspended. He graduated from high school and has worked as a painter for two years fairly successfully. He has been picked up for driving without a license and is now in jail for violating the terms of his probation. He was not drunk when he was picked up.

Two people should read the parts of this script. Then, others may suggest alternative responses using a "Greek chorus" approach, allowing members of the audience to speak for the two readers whenever they become stuck. Try continuing the session without a script.

| | |
|---|---|
| **Counselor:** | Well, I guess you're in some trouble. Why don't you tell me about it? |
| Client: | What's to tell? I was driving to work, and they caught me. I had to get to work somehow. |
| **Counselor:** | You're angry though about being caught. |
| Client: | Damn right. How am I going to get to work if I don't drive? I have to work according to my probation, but they won't let me drive. |
| **Counselor:** | You feel caught in a bind then. |
| Client: | You got it. It's a stupid situation. |
| **Counselor:** | Well, what are you going to do now? |
| Client: | I guess that's why you're here. You're gonna figure it out for me. |
| **Counselor:** | You mean you'd like me to find a solution for you. |
| Client: | I thought that was your job. |
| **Counselor:** | Wait a minute. How do you figure that?  How do you think I'm going to solve this problem for you? |
| Client: | You could talk to my probation officer. |
| **Counselor:** | I suppose I could, but I don't think I will. What do you think needs to be said to your probation officer? |

# Appendix E

## Triangles

Sometimes the most effective way to reach the involuntary client is to work with the members of the client's social system. Usually, when the client is "unmotivated" for treatment, it is because there is someone else around who is "motivated" for him. Parents often polarize around a problem child, for example, with one parent taking the role of disciplinarian, while the other becomes a rescuer and nurturer. Often, then, the route to the identified client is to work with the other parts of the triangle to persuade them neither to rescue nor to arbitrarily punish.

Take a few moments to think about a difficult client. Identify significant others in relationship to the client (including yourself) as they fit into the following roles:

- rescuer

- mediator

- helper

- ally

- disciplinarian

- authority

- persecutor

- victim

# Appendix F

## How People Change

Everyone has a theory about how and why people change. Some counselors believe in the power of cognitions (thinking) to affect behavior. Others think awareness of feelings allows behaviors and thoughts to change. Others believe that thinking and feeling changes follow changes in reinforced behavior.

Imagine that you are developing a treatment program for acting-out adolescents. You want to write a statement on the program's theory of treatment that will be used to conduct staff training and to develop program consistency.

Divide into two groups (if in a classroom setting), one representing treatment staff, the other representing line staff. Each group should write the theory statement from its assigned perspective. (You may wish to add other perspectives, such as the perspective of administration or clients, but it is most important to get the perspective of the treatment team and line staff.) Each group should elect a person to report back to the whole group when it reconvenes. (Suggested time: 30 minutes)

### Suggestions for Writing the Theory Statement:

1. Clearly articulate the mechanism or pathways leading to behavior change. Identify the role of beliefs and thinking, feelings and attitudes, and family and the environment in shaping behavior.

2. It is not sufficient to say "It depends on the situation" when asked how behavior changes. Identify when you might prefer a cognitive approach over an affective approach or behavior modification (or vice versa).

3. Does your theory of behavior change assume:
free will?
conscious choice?
instincts or biological drives?
the powerful influence of early childhood experiences?

When the entire group reconvenes, be prepared to discuss the following:

1. Do treatment and line staff have different theories?

2. Would different perspectives create conflict and reduce treatment effectiveness?

3. How are staff duties affected by the various theoretical models articulated?

4. How would the conduct of individual therapy sessions be different depending on the theory articulated?

# Appendix G

## Exercises to Explore Transference Problems

How might a young African-American male or a Native American male client resist you as a therapist because of your:

- age

- race

- sex

- haircut

- religion

- socioeconomic background

- personality

### Questions

1. How might an alcoholic client resist a counselor who is himself "in recovery"?

2. How might an alcoholic counselor resist a client who is not in recovery?

3. With what personality types do you think you work well? Why?

4. With what personality types do you not work well? Why? What could you do to improve this situation?

# Appendix H

## Sample Test Questions

### Questions for Discussion

1. Involuntary clients seldom are seen in private practices.

    T          F

2. Involuntary clients are always more resistant than voluntary clients.

    T          F

3. Resistance is the same as involuntariness.

    T          F

4. Attempting therapy with unwilling clients:

    a. can't cause any harm
    b. may increase institutional violence
    c. is bad for your blood pressure
    d. none of the above

5. Paradoxical techniques may be useful for:

    a. work with clients in mourning
    b. defiance-based resistance
    c. oppositional-defiant problems
    d. clients with learning disorders
    e. none of the above

6. Transference resistance is the focus of:

    a. brief therapy
    b. solution-focused therapy
    c. dynamic therapy
    d. client-centered counseling

7. Most major decisions:

    a. have conflicting associated emotions
    b. have conflicting associated cognitive structures
    c. are relatively clear cut
    d. none of the above

8. Confrontation is the clear technique of choice for:

    a. successful therapy
    b. work with involuntary clients
    c. work with confused clients
    d. drug and alcohol clients only
    e. all the above
    f. none of the above

## Additional Discussion Questions

1. Describe how your theoretical frame of reference will affect your approach to a treatment-resistant client.

2. List and discuss the major ethical issues on counseling the treatment-resistant client.

3. When should clients be referred for a medical consultation?

4. Explain with what types of clients you are likely to have countertransference reactions?

5. What are the three major areas of resistance?

6. Confrontation is the technique of choice for:

    a. successful therapy
    b. work with involuntary clients
    c. work with confused clients
    d. clients with substance-abuse problems
    e. none of the above

7. Developing empathy with treatment-resistant clients may be difficult due to:

    a. socioeconomic differences
    b. racial differences
    c. disparate beliefs and values between counselors and clients
    d. counselor's dislike of a client
    e. all of the above

8. Why are men more likely to be cynical about counseling than women:

    a. many men see being in counseling as a stigma because they view it as an admission of weakness
    b. they are reluctant to discuss intimate issues with a stranger
    c. they are fearful that divulging information will harm them
    d. they do not see themselves as having a problem
    e. all of the above

9. How can the counselor effectively deal with the issue of male cynicism?

**Answer key to questions 1-8:**
1-F; 2-F; 3-F; 4-b; 5-b and c; 6-e; 7-e; 8-e.

# Appendix I

## Values Clarification Questions

Crime has always fascinated the public. The criminal justice system remains a complex and sometimes confusing collection of police, corrections, and judicial agencies responding to a variety of competing interests and opinions. The following questions are designed to stimulate examination of your values and beliefs about crime and correctional treatment. For the most part, the questions do not have empirically proven right and wrong answers, though there may be some evidence giving credence to certain viewpoints.

1. Do you believe that some criminals are beyond change or rehabilitation and should be permanently incarcerated?

2. Which crime should be punished more severely: child abuse or the embezzlement of $1,000,000? Treason or rape? Would you use different models of therapy for offenders in each category? How would you measure the success of each type of offender?

3. Are crimes considered crimes only because of the way society chooses to define them, or are some acts wrong regardless of cultural context? Does this matter for providing counseling services?

4. Does poverty cause criminal behavior? How does your opinion about this effect how you conduct counseling?

5. Should mentally retarded people be subject to the death penalty? Can a violent mentally retarded person be treated with psychotherapy?

6. If your brother or sister were killed by a drunk driver, do you think you would want a harsher penalty than such offenders currently receive? Could you provide counseling to such a person?

7. What is the most serious crime of all? Should society attempt to rehabilitate these offenders? Are these offenders always antisocial?

8. Do you agree that all defendants should have the right to an attorney? If you were an attorney defending Charles Manson, would you have tried to get him acquitted if there was a technicality or "loophole" in the law that would have accomplished that? Is Charles Manson "rehabilitatable"?

9. Do you think that lawyers who defend a client and accept money they know is illegally gained should be allowed to keep such fees? How would you counsel an attorney who violated the law this way if you had him in treatment?

10. Do you agree with the concept that crimes (felonies) are primarily an offense against the state and that prosecution of such offenses should be a decision not of the victim but of a public prosecutor? How does this view affect your position as a therapist when working with offenders? Do you become an agent of society to protect society against offenders?

11. Do you believe that there is a condition of insanity that impairs people to the extent that they are not responsible for their behavior?

12. Is alcoholism a disease or a behavior that people need to learn to control?

13. Is alcoholism an addiction that is the same as a heroin addiction?

14. Under what circumstances might you hold tobacco companies liable for the damage caused by cigarette smoking? Are tobacco company executives antisocial personalities?

15. Would you object if a group home of mentally retarded people moved into your neighborhood? If it were a halfway house for parolees? If it were a halfway house for teenage substance abusers? If it were a halfway house for psychiatric patients? How would you explain the value of these treatment milieus to neighbors?

16. Should offenders be required to pay for the cost of their treatment during incarceration with money they earn during incarceration?

17. Is work itself "therapeutic" for criminals? Does it directly change criminal behavior?

18. Should parents be required to pay for the incarceration or treatment of their adult children who have become criminals if it can be reasonably demonstrated that the parents contributed to the criminality through poor parenting?

19. Are there certain types of offenses that should disallow an offender from consideration for parole? For probation? For treatment?

20. Do you think some employers mistreat employees so that it justifies some small amounts of employee theft? How would you counsel an employee who had been convicted of theft against an employer from whom you thought the stealing was deserved?

21. If your bank credited your account with $50 that you did not deposit, would you say anything about it? What if it were $500? What if it were $5,000?

22. Why do women commit fewer crimes than men? How does the sex of the client referred by the criminal justice system effect how you conduct therapy?

23. Should an offender who admits guilt receive a lighter sentence than one who denies it? Should offenders be required to admit guilt before being referred for treatment?

24. Should economic crimes, like insider trading, be punished mainly with economic punishments such as fines? Do these offenders have a treatable disorder?

25. Should government officials who knowingly commit crimes not for personal gain but for what they perceive as the good of the country be punished? Should they be referred for counseling?

26. If you were on a jury trying a woman who murdered a man who raped her three months after his crime, would you vote to convict her if it meant she might be executed for her act of revenge? If she were sentenced to prison, how would you begin counseling? What would be your goals for her treatment?

27. A doctor has knowingly overcharged Medicare for a service, but you, the jury, also learn that the doctor provides free services to certain indigent clients. Would you prefer the doctor's punishment be lightened in consideration? If he were given counseling as part of a diversion program, what would be the treatment goals?

28. Would you object if your daughter chose to marry a man who had served time for assault? For robbery? For embezzlement? For shoplifting? For pandering? Would it matter if the person had been in treatment for his problem? How would you know if treatment had been successful? Would you object if your son chose to marry a woman who had served time for assault? Robbery? Embezzlement? Shoplifting? Prostitution?

29. A husband and wife are on trial for the murder of their child, a profoundly mentally and physically handicapped child whose uninsured medical bills were averaging

$10,000 per month. Should this couple be imprisoned for their crime? What kind of psychotherapy do they need? What would be the treatment goals?

30. Do you think the founding fathers would reconsider the concept of "innocent until proven guilty" if they could see what is happening today? What would they think about sending a rapist for psychotherapy?

31. Should corporations that are convicted of acts resulting in loss of human life be given the "death penalty"? For example, if a car manufacturer were convicted of selling a car that executives knew was defective, should the assets of the company be sold and the company killed? Should the executives themselves be tried for murder? Should the executives be required to participate in some type of therapy?

32. Should there be an alternative to imprisonment for tax violators as there is for drunk drivers? That is, should there be a tax compliance school analogous to alcohol safety classes? Would this be therapeutic?

33. Is greed the motivator for most economic crime, from robbery to embezzlement? How do you treat greed?

34. How do you treat the "seven deadly sins": lust, anger, sloth, avarice, pride, envy, gluttony?

35. Is it possible for a battered woman to be so frightened for her safety that she plans and commits murder not out of anger but out of self-defense? How does the notion of personal responsibility and free will fit in with the notion of the battered woman's syndrome?

36. Should rapists be required to take medication that prevents erections as a condition of parole? Is this an ethical form of treatment?

37. If the disproportionate representation of minorities in prison suggests some level of discrimination, does the disproportionate representation of males also suggest some process of discrimination? How should this disparity affect treatment of offenders?

38. How is recognizing cultural diversity related to achieving success when the client is from a different background from the counselor? What adaptations of counseling style and theory may be useful for counseling men from each of the following groups: African-American, Hispanic, Puerto Rican, Thai?

39. Is the concept of justice merely a human invention that has no actual existence outside the human mind?

40. Do you think human society is becoming more or less just and fair? More or less compassionate? More or less rational?

41. Does the world operate on the golden rule (do unto others as you would have them do unto you) or on the rule of gold (those with the gold make the rules)? How do you counsel someone who believes differently from you?

42. Should the drug problem be dealt with: By legalization? By stricter enforcement? By rehabilitation? Other possible solutions?

43. Do you think juveniles who commit felonies should be punished as adults? Should juveniles have more treatment opportunities than adults?

44. Do you think laws should reflect religious values? How do your religious or spiritual values affect therapy with difficult clients?

45. Is a person who has AIDS (or is HIV-positive) but engages in sex anyway guilty of attempted murder? If a client with

AIDS says he intends to sleep with an unknowing person, do you have a duty to warn?

46. Do you believe young black males are more likely than white males to be arrested solely because of their race? How does the race of the client affect how you conduct therapy?

47. Is public humiliation sufficient punishment for some white-collar offenders? Should white-collar offenders be "rehabilitated"?

48. Is it too intrusive to put an electronic device on probationers that allows the probation officer to determine their location at any time? Would it be an invasion of privacy to require probationers to install cameras and/or microphones in their home to allow around-the-clock monitoring? Should a counselor inform the authorities if a client has found a way to defeat the electronic surveillance?

49. Are people becoming less respectful of the rights of others? More cynical about others? What are the causes of this? How does it affect the conduct of psychotherapy?

50. A scientist has developed a device that can be implanted easily inside the inner ear. When activated by remote control, it causes excruciating pain. Would it be ethical to install such devices in prisoners in maximum-security prisons to provide behavior modification consequences?

For workshop information on counseling resistant clients, contact:

New Century Seminars
4901 Main, Suite 400
Kansas City, MO 64112
(816) 756-3552